Social Media

Master Strategies For Social Media Marketing – Facebook, Instagram, TWITTER, YouTube& Linkedin

Noah Hope

© **Copyright 2016 By Noah Hope**

All rights reserved.

In no way is it legal to reproduce, duplicate, or transmit any part of this document in either electronic means or in printed format. Recording of this publication is strictly prohibited and any storage of this document is not allowed unless with written permission from the publisher. All rights reserved.

The information provided herein is stated to be truthful and consistent, in that any liability, in terms of inattention or otherwise, by any usage or abuse of any policies, processes, or directions contained within is the solitary and utter responsibility of the recipient reader. Under no circumstances will any legal responsibility or blame be held against the publisher for any reparation, damages, or monetary loss due to the information herein, either directly or indirectly.

Respective authors own all copyrights not held by the publisher.

Legal Notice:

This book is copyright protected. This is only for personal use. You cannot amend, distribute, sell, use, quote or paraphrase any part or the content within this book without the consent of the author or copyright owner. Legal action will be pursued if this is breached.

Disclaimer Notice:

Please note the information contained within this document is for educational and entertainment purposes only. Every attempt has been made to provide accurate, up to date and reliable complete information. No warranties of any kind are expressed or implied. Readers acknowledge that the author is not engaging in the rendering of legal, financial, medical or professional advice.

Noah Hope

By reading this document, the reader agrees that under no circumstances are we responsible for any losses, direct or indirect, which are incurred as a result of the use of information contained within this document, including, but not limited to, —errors, omissions, or inaccuracies.

Social Media

Table of Contents

Page

INTRODUCTION..7

CHAPTER 1: WHAT IS SOCIAL MEDIA MARKETING?..9

CHAPTER 2: THE BENEFITS OF SOCIAL MEDIA MARKETING..17

CHAPTER 3: FACEBOOK..21

CHAPTER 4: TWITTER..53

CHAPTER 5: INSTAGRAM......................................73

CHAPTER 6: YOUTUBE..93

CHAPTER 7: LINKEDIN..115

CHAPTER 8: SOCIAL MEDIA MARKETING TIPS..135

CHAPTER 9: LAW OF SOCIAL MEDIA MARKETING..149

CHAPTER 10: SOCIAL MEDIA MARKETING MYTHS..153

CONCLUSION..157

Social Media

Introduction

I want to thank you and congratulate you for downloading the book, "Social Media: Master Strategies for Social Media Marketing – Facebook, Instagram, Twitter& YouTube".

This book contains an overview of what social media marketing is and how to create a social media marketing strategy. Social media marketing has become a necessary role in business advertising. More than three billion people are now utilizing the worldwide web, which means internet sales are continuing to climb. Building an online presence is becoming vital for businesses. This book will outline the key elements that make up your social media marketing strategy as well as the benefits of using social media platforms.

The book also takes a deeper look into Facebook, Instagram, Twitter& YouTube to ensure you have the skills you need to build your online presence, build user engagement, and grow your business like never before.

Thanks again for downloading this book, I hope you enjoy it!

Social Media

Chapter 1
What is Social Media Marketing?

Social media marketing is the utilization of modern social media platforms such as Facebook, Twitter, Instagram, YouTube, LinkedIn, and others to gain website traffic and bring attention to your brand as well as expand your marketing communication. There are several reasons why you may want to expand your marketing resources into social media, but to understand the significance and importance of that expansion, below are some statistics that might baffle you.

There are over 2.3 billion social media user accounts on the worldwide web

176 million people created new social media accounts in 2015

Businesses earned $8.3 million from advertising on social media platforms in 2015

B2B marketers are generating over half of their leads from social media

Over 70% of the users on Twitter that follow a brand end up making future purchases

Online buying decisions are 93% dependent on social media

It is predicted that B2B marketers will spend over $100 billion in advertising on social media by 2017

As you can see advertising and marketing have taken a turn in the last several years with the emergence of social media. There are too many users online not to take advantage of this avenue. The benefits of spending more on social media advertising and less on traditional advertising will maximize your marketing strategy. As people shy away from conventional advertising, be it flyers, billboards, orTV commercials, more and more companies are looking to advertise online and within social media. All you have to do to see this change is look how Netflix is bringing down cable companies, DVR boxes that allow customers to fly through TV commercials, and apps for just about everything. Bills do not have to come through the mail any longer, with online billing options for nearly every single bill you will receive. Why would anyone want to receive something paper when they can easily scroll past interesting facts, companies and promotions on their Facebook, Twitter, Instagram, or LinkedIn feed?

As you plan your social media marketing strategy, you need to look at all of the platforms available. What is the popularity like, what marketing opportunities are there, what type of content will you need to create and share, and do you have the right content that will be engaging enough to generate leads and purchases? Taking advantage of every social media platform available to you may be the best option for you and your company, or it may be beneficial just to use one or two platforms.

Social Media Marketing Strategy

Your social media marketing strategy should clearly identify your business goals. You need to have a clear vision of what you are working towards so that you can create objectives to attain them. Your goals may be to increase brand awareness, retain your customers, introduce new products or services, expand to a new geographic or demographic market; etc. Choose two or three primary goals that you believe are attainable from your list, as well as two or three secondary goals that you want to focus on in this marketing strategy.

Once you have your goals clearly defined, you can then develop specific measures to achieve those goals. Ask yourself how you can meet those goals. If one of your primary goals is to increase brand awareness, what can you feasibly do to meet that goal? Use Facebook advertising and contests? Generate Twitter posts on a routine basis? Whatever the objectives are you should be able to meet the goal successfully in a timely manner. Your goals should be specific, measurable, achievable, relevant and time-bound. Note: Do not overshoot your goals. For example, do not set a goal that you will reach over one million users on social media within the first year. This is highly unfeasible and unrealistic. Make sure your goals are relevant and consistent with your company's mission.

Using social media as a marketing tool is a great way to heighten your brand awareness and tap into new users, especially the younger market. However, social media marketing is a long-term goal and takes a lot of time and effort to achieve high-standing status. Be patient with your goals and re-assess what they mean to you and your company monthly, if not weekly.

After you have your goals and objectives, you then need to identify who you need to engage. Who are your customers? Who will use your product or services? You need to think about your target audience from every perspective including, but not limited to demographics, geography, age, income, occupation, motivations, obstacles, etc. The more specific you can breakdown your user groups, the better off you will be when it comes time to market your brand. You will be able to target specific groups and tailor your advertising for them.

Now that you know your audience, what does your competition look like? Take an active approach in studying your competition to understand what social media platforms they are currently using and what type of content seems to attract the most response. You can use these notes as you decide what social media platforms you believe will be the most beneficial for you and the kind of content you need to post to be successful. The most important thing you need to remember is that engagement is your number one goal. If you are posting daily on any social media platform, or perhaps all of them, but are not getting any engagement, or very little, it's time to re-think your plans. Go over your goals, see what others are doing, and re-start your social media marketing.

Once you find out what seems to be working for your competitors and you have done your research to determine what will work best for your business (remember your research should be based on your goals and objectives as well what works for your competitors), it is time to decide what social media platforms you will use. I will tell you that most people spend at least 40% of their online time on Facebook and at least 20% of their time on Twitter. These two platforms are almost a given for any new social media marketing campaign.

You can also use one form of social media more frequently than the other. Say, for example, you focus more energy on Facebook, and post a little less on Twitter. You're still reaching an audience and putting your name out there, but you are focusing your efforts on one social media platform more than you are in another. You can also increase the time and money spent on other platforms as you continue to grow and feel comfortable using social media for marketing. A simple way to even out the amount of time you are spending on your platforms is to link your accounts. For instance, you can link your Facebook and Twitter accounts, so that when you post something on one, it will automatically post to the other.

Once you have settled on your social media platforms, you need to develop your content strategy. Content is extremely important to building relationships online. Your new accounts will be meaningless unless you have meaningful content to connect you with new followers (either current customers or prospective customers). Your content strategy will include what content you will post, the timing of your posts and the frequency you should be posting. There are different types of content that can be posted: pure text, images, links, video, etc. All of these have their own value, which will be discussed later on.

Now that the entire social media marketing strategy has been written, it is time to allocate some time and resources to this plan. You need to decide how much money you are willing to allocate to the social media side of advertising as opposed to traditional advertising. Many companies are pulling advertising dollars from other advertising budgets; however, many have now created a special budget for social media because of its impact on the company. You will need to look at your return on investment to help you make these decisions and it maybe something that comes alive as you generate profits. Maybe you build the social media marketing strategy over time. Your budget may need to be broadened the longer you market with social media and use different ways to engage your customers and future customers. Also, who will handle this new advertising burden? Do you have a social media expert(s)? Make sure you have a plan intact that controls who is developing the content, researching content, posting the content, and handing the management of each site. This may be a job for someone who can handle more responsibility, meeting with yourself to figure out your marketing plan. Or, you may need to hire an entirely new person (or promote from within and hire for their previous position) to help take over the social media platforms. Once you get going and use each one, a job that once seemed flippant and easy will take great time and care.

This entire process should be a work in process as you build your social media marketing strategy. Ultimately, it will be as successful as you make it. This book is designed to give you the tools you need to make each social media platform as successful as possible. I present chapters about specific social media platforms that will outline tools and features to help you generate more leads and user engagement, as well as tools to help manage the platform more easily.

Social Media

Chapter 2
The Benefits of Social Media Marketing

We have already discussed the importance of social media, but what about the benefits that social media has to offer? On a personal level, social media can be more about a personality contest and who gets the most likes and comments. From a business perspective, social media has an exorbitant amount of benefits. Some of those benefits include an increase in traffic to their websites, increase in loyal fans, improved search rankings, an increase in business partnerships, improved sales, a reduction in overall marketing expenses, and much more. A couple of the top benefits are explained in more detail below.

First and foremost, the biggest benefit is exposure. The number of people a business can reach online is far more than they can reach face-to-face. This means that brand awareness can increase simply by sharing and promoting the brand online. In fact, most people look for product reviews and product information online prior to purchasing it. While a lot of people would look towards a website first instead of calling, or just dropping by the store, people are now looking towards social media. With just a scroll through Instagram you can find great deals and new events without heading to a website or inquiring. If a person is not in the community, they may not know what you are offering. Bring in social media and you can increase your customer base to just outside your community and further, building a relationship with those who know you and who will get to know you. This is why utilizing social media as a marketing campaign is so meaningful. By becoming more involved with the customer, you are building loyalty.

Social media sites help develop a brand and legitimize them in ways that regular websites cannot. While static webpages tell consumers who they are, provide a little bit of background, and provide a shopping area, they do not change much. Social media sites allow companies to establish themselves as industry leaders. They can showcase their products and services, provide question and answer sessions, and continually produce updates to provide more about their brand. Building credibility is an important part of social media marketing.

Social media is invaluable to customer service. Many customers tend to use social media as a way to communicate with businesses. Either to ask questions, compliment them or complain. Use this to your advantage by ensuring you respond to your messages and posts within a reasonable amount of time. Large companies such as Nike, T-Mobile, and Under Armor are likely to see over 2,000 questions on their wall at any given time because they have well over a million followers. It is important that they keep customer service agents focused on social media sites and answer at least 65% of these questions because recent studies show that 1 in 3 people prefer social media contact rather than phone calls. The better you serve your customers, regardless of the avenue, the better your brand appearance is. In today's society people are using social media as a primary means of communication. Gone are the days of calling in to complain, or scroll through lists of reviews. Now, all anyone has to do is take to social media to see how a business stands up. Take this into consideration as you build your online presence.

Social media marketing is a big driver of increased sales and profit. There are numerous tools and features on each of the social media platforms that help drive consumers to a sale. The ability to buy directly from a shop on Facebook, create target driven advertising campaigns, buy directly from Amazon or Twitter, use Instagram as a place to introduce your followers to more than just your store, and YouTube for a look at how you might use products or services. The future is lazy and instant, if you do not keep up, you'll be driven out. There are a million tools and features that can be capitalized on from each of the social media platforms available. The key is finding which ones will work for your company.

Last, social media marketing can reduce your overall advertising and marketing costs. Social media is a cost-effective manner of getting your brand and message out because of the population pool that social media platforms have. You have the ability to get text, images, videos, etc. in various forms of promotions, showcases, product updates and so on free of charge as often as you like. The use of paid ads using target audiences (and management of your social media accounts) is where you will invest your money. Social media campaigns are highly specific and more cost-effective than any TV ad or radio ad you have produced before.

If you're still using your original ways of advertising and want to add social media to the mix, this can be a great tool. Customers will see you everywhere, from TV to radio to Twitter to Facebook. By using a smaller amount of money to access social media, and still keeping your original advertising, at least for the time being, you will find that your budgets will start to look healthier. In essence, you are getting the best bargain possible by using social media and are accessing the largest population available to you.

Chapter 3
Facebook

Facebook is important to your social media marketing strategy because it has more users than any other social media platform with roughly 62% of its users logging on daily. What better way to engage with people than the largest worldwide web platform? Facebook is becoming a central hub for the worldwide web because of its integration with many other websites. It is in your best interest to invest some time and money into Facebook. Take some time to prepare a marketing strategy that will focus on your page, what ads you will create and who you will target, what groups you may want to join and/or create, and how you will market yourself.

Your Facebook Page Setup

The first thing you need to do is set up your Facebook page. The first thing you will need to do is choose the category. Facebook allows you to choose from six different categories:

Local Business or Place

Company, Organization or Institution

Brand or Product

Artist, Band or Public Figure

Entertainment

Cause or Community

Once you have selected your category, you can select an industry-specific category. Then you will get into filling out some details about your business such as your website address, contact information (address and phone number,), a description about your business, upload a profile picture, etc.

You really need to focus on filling out the 'About' section. Do not leave your contact details blank because this is how your customers or potential customers will be able to reach you. You do not want them searching for contact information. Contact information needs to be readily available for ease. People are using social media as a way to find out information quicker and easier. Making it hard for them to find out information about your company, especially the most important – contact information – will hurt your ratings. You need to provide a short description that will be used during search results on search engines such as Google, and you need a longer description that provides more detailed information about your business. The description can be information about why you went into business, what your products and services intend to do, what you offer, your price range, your hours of business, parking information, etc. The more you provide, the easier it is for your viewers to understand your business. Remember, although many people will head to your website afterward, there are still many others who will be treating your Facebook page as your website. Upload as much information about yourself as possible, including reviews. Think of the 'About' section of your Facebook page as similar to that of the 'About' section on your own website. What are customers going to be looking for? Is there anything you need to specifically say? The cleaner, more professional and intriguing your Facebook page looks, the more leads that will turn into customers will roll through. Also, make sure you upload a profile picture and cover photo that represent your business. Typically, this should be a logo or something that truly represents your business. Your images need to be identifiable with your brand.

Types of Marketing Content for Facebook

Poll Feature

Facebook polling is a perfect way to engage users. You set up the polls with customizable forms that are accessible on all devices including mobile phones and tablets. The hope is that you can expand your reach beyond your current followers by sharing the poll.

It is a paid for feature ($8 per month for a subscription) that allows you to create up to 40 customizable questions with images and/or videos to make it more interactive. You can achieve even more likes by using the referral contest feature. A referral contest simply provides participants with a chance to win something if they refer the contest to friend. Once that friend participates via invitation, they are eligible for the prize. It is a win-win for everyone involved.

The poll allows you to track the origin of participation whether it's by invitation from you, your wall, a friend, a friend's wall, or link shared. You can all see charted results at the end of the pool on a dashboard that is fully exportable. It is an easy and fun feature to get some engagement and conversation flowing on your page.

Special Promotions and Coupons

A lot of people like and follow a brand's Facebook and Twitter pages because they hope to receive special incentives and offers. It is a great idea to post special promotions your business maybe offering, or coupons every once in a while, to keep those people coming back and to entice new people to follow your page. Promotions and coupons are things people love to get on Facebook. You do not have to have promotions or coupons all of the time, but every once in a while, it is a great way to give back to your customers and followers. Putting up a post about special promotions and coupons can help you achieve greater leads. You can post special promotions that only your Facebook followers would get. Do not post these on your other social media accounts, which will take away from the theme here. Instead, offer incentives to only those who follow you, or will follow you. People love to feel special, and this is a great way to show them that you value them as a customer.

While posting specific promotions and coupons that are available solely to your followers is a great way to stay in touch with them and make them feel special, you can also use promotions in Facebook ads. This will open up to a wider array of Facebook users, and can result in leads pouring in. This is a great tool to use if you're going through a slow period of sales and want to ramp up the sales margins.

Announcements, Pricing and New Products/Services

Facebook is the perfect place to announce events, special programs, pricing changes or new products and services. As discussed earlier in this book, you will reach a large volume of people on Facebook, so it is worth it to you to post important messages such as those. Some may feel like they're annoying Facebook users by posting a lot on their page, but if they're following you, they're waiting for content to be readily available. If you have a special Memorial Day event coming up, it is a good idea to post a weekly update letting people know you are preparing for the big event. Provide details and updates as you get closer to the event, this will get everyone excited and gives you the opportunity to promote to a wide range of people. Do not overwhelm people by posting more than once a week regarding this specific event, unless the event is that week. Put up a post at the beginning of the week to remind everyone of the event, or that a new product is coming in, and then put up another post that day to help promote the event or product. People love to hear about events and new products, even if they are not interested in that particular one at that time. You have to give social media marketing time, as the leads coming through won't always be successful on each post, ad, or announcement. Social media marketing is a long-term strategy.

Testimonials

Testimonials are one of the greatest ways to get engagement on your Facebook page and collect bragging rights. For every satisfied customer, get them to send you a written testimonial that you can then use as a Facebook post. If you can, snap a photo of them with the product (or have them send it in themselves), or even create a video testimonial with yourself and your customers! This is a fantastic way to let future customers know that customer satisfaction is your number one priority. Make the post interesting and intriguing for people to view, and tag your customer in the post so they can start the branching effect out of Facebook's timeline.

Link to Blog Posts or Your Website

A lot of people use Facebook as a type of news outlet. You can get information from numerous news sites directly to one newsfeed without having to hop to each website, or pay costly membership fees. Putting up your own information can add to the benefits for your customers. It is always a good idea to link to outside blogs that you have and your website (and vice versa). It is important to keep all of your websites connected.

Facebook is only good for limited content, so your blog allows you to expand on longer stories, product descriptions or usage, industry specific information that relates to your products or services, etc. Not only does it engage users on Facebook with your actual website and everything that you offer, be it promotions, events, products, or tips, but it can help with your website traffic. Creating an organic SEO can take hours to get yourself at the top of Google. If you continuously link your blog posts and website content to your Facebook page, users will engage and continuously head over to your website, inching your website closer and closer to the number one spot.

Link to other Content or Media

Linking to outside content or media can be invaluable. If you found a video or article that is relevant to your business or industry that is interesting, why not share it? You might be surprised at the amount of responses you get. What about a new way to use one of your products? People will be ecstatic that you shared a video of a customer tutorial. This is also a great way to share with your Facebook followers that you also have a YouTube channel. Sharing content from other websites and other great businesses that you want to help promote is great, but sharing content from your own social media platforms and/or website is a perfect way to link all of your marketing strategies together. The more value you can add to your page the better your engagement will be. How-to videos, industry-specific regulations, and changes that customers may want to see in the future, etc. Any value added content is good content. Letting Facebook users see something other than your business, or just tips from your view and your products every day can get a bit boring, no matter how much they love your services. Putting in content that is outside of your business, but still linked to your industry, is a great way to add a little bit more engagement with your Facebook page, turning those leads into customers and customers into money.

Videos

Videos are great marketing tools for business. News outlets are even turning to posting more videos on their online newspapers, engaging the masses with the type of medium that they prefer. So why not try your hand at making your own marketing videos and getting your name out there? There are some rules to remember, though. Make sure your videos are inspirational and not overly salesy. It is a proven fact that inspirational videos will get a more positive response than sales videos. Humans are emotional creatures, so speaking from the heart will speak more to a person than pitching a sales speech. Next, provide your audience with some educational perspective because most of us like to learn. Create videos that teach us something useful and provide us with valuable information that is engaging. Third, you must be entertaining. Humor will speak to people more than anything else. However, offering a glimpse of behind the scenes footage into how your business runs and about your team can be just as effective. We are curious creatures by nature and like to know who we are working with and buying from. Besides, seeing what your favorite celebrity or your favorite company is doing (besides selling you something) is entertaining. It's fun to see what the business is doing behind-the-scenes. Give us some information about your business and your team. You will be surprised at the response you get.

One advantage of videos is that you can get a lot of engagement right away. Videos on Facebook now automatically play as you scroll past, but are muted, letting people view them quickly to see if they would like to see more. By using a video that engages the user from the start, perhaps by using props or a big opening scene, you can get a much higher engagement. Everyone likes to look at something that looks entertaining and fun, or peaks their interest, so taking the time to really craft your opening scene can play out well for you in the end. You can also try using Featured Videos, uploaded daily, weekly, monthly, whatever works for you and your customer base. People love to tune into the things that only they want to view, and by getting similar content and more information on a topic, you will create great user engagement. Another great way to get more views for Facebook Videos is to try using the call-to-action button on your Facebook page. This button allows you to post a scene or a specifically designed poster for your video, and will take the user to your desired video platform, be it your YouTube channel or your website.

Although not available to everyone, another great video feature that Facebook is rolling out is Live Video Broadcasting. By using livestream on Facebook, you can connect with users by streaming an event, or a webinar/promotion while it's happening. You can get subscribers to your Live Video Broadcasting, which is a great way to see how many people are interested in your Live Video feeds, gaining more subscribers as the masses join the few. If you're going to try Live Video Broadcasting, make sure to let the public know that you will be doing a Live Video next week, another post at the beginning of that week, and then put out a post that day reminding followers that they can tune in. You should continue doing these posts even as your subscribers multiply, continuously adding new subscribers to your list and letting other Facebook users know about your video(s). Pro tip: make sure your internet connection is strong. This is not the time to be posting Live Videos from your lake with the touch-and-go service. You do not want your followers and subscribers thinking that you cannot put out a proper video.

Scripting is key even though this video will be live. You do not want to go in without knowing at least a little bit of what you're going to say. Write up a great introduction to your video that those who are just tuning in can read. Make this as intriguing as possible to gain more subscribers, followers, and views. Do not forget to introduce yourself to your viewers before starting your video, each and every time. No matter how famous you are, it is always courteous to introduce yourself. You can make this simpler as time goes on and as you gain more followers and subscribers.

Many people may start to comment on your video as you are shooting, so take the time to read the comments and answer any questions or concerns that they may have. They may even have great ideas for new videos for you to produce next week. The more often you post, and the longer the video(s), the more possible viewers you may engage with. Make a schedule and take the time to think about what you will be covering in your Live Video Broadcast. Maybe you will be doing a How-To Video or a walk around your office. A great video down the road once you have a few subscribers under your belt is to address your viewers and answer all of their questions, either from previous videos or in real-time from this video. Videos are fun, easy and a great way to gain exposure in social media.

Share Photos

Facebook is a great place to share photos. In fact, as a business it is an ideal location for introducing new products, sharing photos of customers using your products, and even balancing out the advertising with pictures of your business family. Post pictures from a company retreat or event, casual pictures from around the office, pictures of your business at local events, and anything else that adds to the business environment. Your employees are an extension of your brand, so use them when you can.

It is also important to post shareable photos. By this I mean post images that people want to share. Make it something that is funny, interesting, valuable, and worth someone's time. Another great way to get your users to engage in your photos is getting them to post photos of themselves using your products, or any that you have that were submitted by customers. You can urge them to share these photos with their friends and family.

Also, make sure you tag people in your photos whether it is other organizations or individuals. This is another great way to get your photos circulating the Facebook world.

Last, post photos as often as you can, the more you post, the more people will see. It is one of the best ways to engage people and advertise your brand.

Newsletter Signup

Newsletter signups are a fantastic way to generate leads. By asking your followers to sign up for your monthly newsletter, you can collect their email addresses so that you can later send them coupons, news, special promotion information, offers, new product information, etc. These are all items that people are willing to receive in exchange for providing their email address. You can also entice them to sign up by providing an initial offer as well. Newsletters can be a very effective lead generating campaign. Make sure that your newsletter is both informative and entertaining to keep people opening and engaging with your content.

Building Your Community

Once you have developed your Facebook page and have begun the process of promoting your page, there are several things you need to do to build your community. First, after you have 25 fans, you can setup your customized URLs sure you claim your Facebook URL so that you can start associating it with your business. You can customize your URL to something that fits your business model. For example, use your business name. It needs to be unified with your business model so that all of your websites and social media platforms correlate nicely. This is an easy way to get Google to pick you out of the masses when someone searches for your name. Keeping your URL unique, but similar to your website will link everything together, bringing you closer to the top of the search page.

Focus on getting more fans. You do this by promoting your new Facebook page by word of mouth, signage at your business, on your website, flyers, menus, packaging and shopping bags, or even mailings that go out to your current customers. Start inviting your friends to like your page, like related businesses and like industry-specific businesses, like content of other business, invite other businesses to connect, post shareable content as discussed in the previous section, post upcoming events on your page, and start sharing promotions. Remember to focus on the content that you post as discussed previously. Post photos, events, links, quotes and graphics, product descriptions, images of your business, and videos. Do not forget to tag those who are in the photos. If you hold an event and tag customers and their friends in the uploaded photo, they can share it with their own friends, garnering the branch out effect of Facebook's timeline. If any of those who are following you or are friends with you are in any photos, or if they are interested in any products and/or services from your company, share your specific post onto their timeline. Their friends will be able to see this, starting that branching out effect again. Start interacting with your customers through polls and questions and be as responsive as you can when they do engage. Schedule your posts on a weekly basis so that you know exactly when and what you are going to post. By posting on a consistent basis, you are influencing engagement.

Use Facebook tabs to your advantage by linking to your other social media accounts, create a shop on Facebook (talked about in more detail below), embed a signup form for your newsletter, include fun customizable contests and sweepstakes, and add your business information so that people can 'check in' at your business.

Tools and Features Offered

Cover Photo

This may seem like a no-brainer for those who regularly use Facebook, and doesn't look like a big feature for marketing. However, changing your cover photo, as well as your profile picture, every so often can increase engagement with your Facebook company page. If you have a specific logo as your background, that's a great start. Try changing it up to a team photo, a photo of your shop or warehouse, or a temporary profile picture of one of your featured products. This can let everyone know about the featured product, it will show up on their timeline and will get those who have been quiet to take another look at your Facebook page again.

Facebook Insights

Facebook Insights is a tool that Facebook offers to you after you receive 30 fan likes. Page managers are provided with statistics to see what the activity level is like on their page. You are presented with statistics that help you learn more about your audience. You are given general statistics about you page (number of fans, how many new fans you have, if your engagement has increased or decreased, the viewing habits of your viewers, etc.) and then more specific statistics broken down by post.

You can see what posts you have made incurred the most engagement including the most likes, comments, and shares. You can see how many people your post reached, who clicked on the post, and how many people reacted to it. These can also be broken down by post type: posts, photos, videos, and links. Insights also lets you know when your followers are actually on Facebook. Insights provides statistical information for creating target audience ads and when to promote those ads. The information you obtain helps you understand your audience better. The more you understand your audience, the better marketing content you can create and promote.

Call-to-Action Button

Facebook's Call-to-Action button is a way to link your business's most important objectives on or off Facebook in an easy manner. For example, contacting you is an important function that many customers come to your Facebook page to do. Facebook has made this even easier by making a Contact Us Call-to-Action button. No longer do customers have to hunt and peck for your contact details. A simple click of a button and they can contact you. Facebook offers seven call-to-actions: Book Now, Contact Us, Use App, Play Game, Shop Now, Sign Up and Watch Video.

Book Now can be used to book new appointments directly from your page. Shop Now allows you to create a Facebook shop where customers can shop directly off of Facebook without ever having to leave making getting a sale even easier. Sign Up is an easy way to get followers to sign up for a Newsletter. All of the call-to-action buttons can be used effectively to engage your customers and keep them from leaving your Facebook page. This is a great tool to effectively tie in your outside websites and communicate between all of your web interfaces. In essence, the buttons are for communicating to your audience, to drive traffic to your other sites or provide an easy way to get your customers to do 'something' – perform some action.

Pin Posts to your Timeline

Make sure that you do not forget that you can pin posts to the top of your page. When you pin posts to the top of your page, those posts will be the very first post that followers will see when they visit your page, until you unpin them.

Pinning posts is a fantastic marketing technique when you have large events coming up, if you have sale events, promotions or new products/services. For example, let's say that you have a huge sale event coming up for the Labor Day holiday. You may want to create a nice image that states when the event will be, what the discounts will be, how long it will last, etc. Make it readable, flashy, and shareable so that when you post it followers will want to read it and share it. Plus, when new people visit your page they will not scroll on by it as it will be the very first post on your page.

To pin a post at the top of your page, make the post, load the image, and after it has been saved and posted then click on the downward-facing arrow on the top right-hand corner of the post. From the drop-down menu, select 'Post to Top'. That post will now stay at the top of your page until you unpin it. Pinning posts is a wonderful advertising tool to use for any business owner.

Facebook Ads

Facebook Ads is unique in the sense that you can reach target audiences. You have the ability to show ads to a specific set of people based on their age, gender, geographic location, interests, and more. This is perfect as you can send out advertising to show up on someone's newsfeed that would be most likely to buy your product, join your team, or become a future customer. It does not matter what your end goal is, Facebook will help you generate an ad. To start, Facebook asks you to choose your goal based on the following options:

Talk about your Page and posts (Boost your posts)

Connect with your business on Facebook (Promote your Page)

Go to your website (Send people to your website)

Shop or take action on your website (Increase engagement in your app)

Install or use your app (Get installs of your app)

Shop in your store (Reach people near your business)

Invite others to your events (Raise attendance at your event)

Redeem offers (Get people to claim your offer)

Get video views *NEW on Facebook

Then you select an image or a set of images to associate with your ad and give your campaign a name. When you are posting photos with your ad set, which is highly recommended, make sure that your photo doesn't contain 20% or more of text. Facebook will automatically reject your ad, causing you wasted time and money, which can cause frustration within your company, especially if you are hiring someone to make up a specific logo or banner ad. If your logo itself has too much wording, look into making up a specific one just for Facebook ads. This gives you the opportunity to make a simple logo that can be used in smaller ads, or as your Google URL logo as well. Instead of using your photos for all of your call-to-action text, use the headline and description boxes to help bring attention to your ad. These will go above and below your ad image, providing details to your ad.

Last, you will begin selecting your audience. Here is where you can select a location, age range, gender, language, behaviors, etc. allowing you to narrow in on who you want to focus on for a particular ad. If you have a specific audience picked out already, that's great. You can also upload your e-mail contact list onto Facebook to target audiences that are already your clients, or who are potential clients. This is a great tool to use, bringing more awareness to your business to people who would be more likely to refer you to their friends and family.

If your ad has been running for a while and your budget needs to change, or you see that it is not performing that well, you can always go in and edit the lifetime or daily budget (depending on which one you chose) and the end date of your ad. If you want your ad to run for one more day, but want the daily amount to be doubled, simply increase the daily amount and set the end date for 24 hours later. You can always change the exact time an ad will end, which can come in handy. If an ad is set to end before 9:00am the following day, you should push it to at least 10:30am in order to gain more views. People look at their phones and log onto Facebook early in the morning when they first arrive to work and before their day gets busier.

The ad tool also provides you with analytics to help you understand how your ads performed and what you can do to improve your reach and engagement. The best way to increase engagement on your Facebook page, your ads, and your overall lead generation, is to use the 'send people to your website' option. You can post your photo(s) or video(s) with a description, a call-to-action and watch as the leads roll in. This may not work for every single ad set, and you will have to play around with a few different ideas. Try making an ad set with the same features and targets, but with different wording and photo(s). Then, track your impressions (whether or not anyone liked it, commented, or shared your ad), the money spent and how many clicks to your website were generated. If one ad is performing better than the other, get rid of one ad and continue on. Try making up a few different ads, even if one is working well. You do not want the same ad running through Facebook newsfeeds for months on end. People will get tired of seeing the same ad and get fed up with you and your company, or they may assume you are making no new developments or products. Instead, switching up which ads you use will help keep users engaged with you, your company and any promotions, products or events you may have going on.

You can use Facebook ads to help promote a certain product, get more people to an event, or just let everyone know a little more about your business and gain exposure. Mixing up the different ads, with one running to gain exposure while another features a certain product, then swapping with an event ad or other great products, will keep people excited to actually see these ads and engage with them.

Remember that there may be a lot of comments on your ads, some good and some bad. Make sure you reply back to these comments and any messages that may come your way to increase engagement with your Facebook page and your overall social media and business appearance. When you're using social media as a platform for marketing in business, your social media presentation is linked to your business one.

Facebook ads are a very powerful tool to help increase your engagement and revenue stream. You can make ads for anything, be it events, new products, a sale, or your brand in general. Use ads to generate more leads, clicks to your website, views, whatever you had chosen above. Use it to your advantage and use target audiences to effectively market your business.

Campaigns and Contests

Facebook also allows you to run many different campaigns and contests. There are third-party applications that make this even easier with themes and management utilities that help manage winners and the promotion aspect of each contest. You can run contests such as sweepstakes, picture contests, referral promotions, essay contests, photo captions, video contests, music contests, and polling.

These contests can be based on an action so that a user must do something in order to get access to your campaign. For example, in order to write a caption for your photo caption contest, they must follow you on Facebook. To enter into a sweepstakes program, users must enter their email address into a form first, which generates email leads for you. Polling allows you to find out more about your followers. Use this one for fun, but also use it as a way to get to know your audience.

People love to win free stuff and will get involved if there's the possibility of free product or money on the line. By giving away free product over social media, you will be able to engage with your followers, and other Facebook users, on another level and will get a great amount of e-mails or followers for lead generation. If your goal is to get followers on your Facebook page, set it up, so they have to follow you in order to participate. If it's to simply gain more leads, use the e-mail given to sign them up for a newsletter or send them a friendly e-mail thanking them for signing up for the promotion. There are many different routes and ideas that you can use to make your campaign or contest successful, bringing in both leads and letting you get involved with future customers.

Management and Reporting

There are numerous management tools available to help you with scheduling posts. You can set up post queuing that will allow you to have the posts ready as much as a week to a month ahead of time. These can be pure text posts, images, videos, contests, etc. You can also have each post target a set audience. The posts will be set up to post at a specific time of day on a certain day. This is a great feature to use so you can still post information, photos, and videos to your Facebook page outside normal office hours. This feature can help make it seem like there's someone constantly manning your account, updating and posting at all hours of the day, allowing you to save money on hiring someone for weekend and evening shifts to look after your social media account. You can also go into your post and edit if you need to add more information if the information has changed or if you made a mistake.

Reporting is also a feature that is extremely useful for businesses. There are analytical tools much like Facebook Insights available that can provide you with valuable information and reports about your user engagement, average response rates, page likes, follower change rates, and comparison tools that provide you with comparison data. You can view information about your competitor's pages such as what advertising might be working for them, their reach rates, engagement information, etc. You also have the option to see what your ad campaign value is. There are all sorts of reporting and statistics available; it is up to you to choose what is best for you. Do your research and find out what tools are best for you.

Problems With Advertising on Facebook

Besides all of the previously mentioned advantages that Facebook offers to clients who are interested in advertising on their pages, the advertising on Facebook also has certain disadvantages. The following part of this book will deal with certain disadvantages in relation to the advertising on Facebook. The following will also serve as guidance for you and your business as well as an example of what you can expect when advertising on Facebook in negative context.

Interaction with people or customers is one of the crucial aspects of any kind of marketing. Facebook advertising is not different in any aspect only in this case interaction is done online and without face – to – face contact between the client or the customer and the business owner. Since Facebook is an open network in a sense that almost everybody can use it there are those kinds of people who will use your Facebook page, ad, post or anything related to your business to post bad comments or reviews expressing their opinion without even being customer of your business. Since it is not possible to control what people do or write on Facebook your business ads on Facebook or your page will be open to people comments who only want to offend you or your business or evaluate your business as bad. It seems unrealistic to expect all positive reviews or comments on your business and because of that you have to ready to answer to such comments by reliable arguments which will in response generate more positive comments from other people who do not share the same opinion as the people who negatively commented your posts or your business. Some Facebook users might even post false allegations that can badly influence your business unless you do not take care and respond on such allegations. It seems hard for small businesses to monitor every comment and opinion expressed about your business because such job demands people who are constantly online on Facebook and who are reviewing and responding to such comments. Small businesses often cannot afford that kind of employees and because of that many allegations and comment remain unanswered and in such a negative image about your business can be created. When people see negative comments about anything and especially about certain businesses those negative comments remain in their memory more often than it is a case with positive comments. In case of negative comments as well as in the case of positive comments you will never be able to see the number of people who saw those comments and because of that you might neglect such comments without even realizing that the number of people affected by such comment may have big negative effect on your business.

Another, we may say, problem with advertising on Facebook is the fact that when someone clicks "like" on your page it does not mean that he or she will receive or see all updates on your Facebook page. In order to receive or see updates from your Facebook page, or for you to interact with Facebook users, Facebook users must be subscribed to your page. The number of people who liked your page might be big, but in fact, the number of people who actually see what you post on your Facebook page might be dramatically smaller. Even more dramatic case occurs when Facebook users unsubscribe from your Facebook page. Even though they might still like you page, after unsubscribing, the things you post on your page will be hidden from the news feed of the Facebook users. In order for people who unsubscribed from your page to see what you are posting they need to go on to your Facebook page directly and there see what is going on with your business. However, this kind of interaction happens very rarely because when people are not receiving or seeing post from your page it might easily happen that your business will become forgotten by Facebook users. With all of this being said it is clear that it is impossible for you to know how many people actually saw or interacted with your posts or your page.

Another big issue with the advertising on Facebook is definitely the price of such advertising. There are two types of prices for advertising on Facebook. One type of price is called 'a cost per click' or CPC and the other is called 'cost per impressions' or CPM. The minimum price of CPC in relation to Facebook advertising is $0.01, and the minimum price of CPM is $0.02. Even from the moment you create your Facebook page, and you want to pay for advertising Facebook will offer you advice to go higher on those prices and to choose to pay more for your advertising. This happens because businesses or pages that pay more for Facebook advertising are shown more on the people's news feeds around the planet while those business that pay less are less likely for their post or adverts to reach widespread audience. From all of this we can conclude that big businesses and companies have huge advantage in comparison to small businesses because it is easier for big companies to pay more for advertising unlike smaller companies who have problems with such high prices for advertising because that would mean losing a huge amount of their income on advertising without even being sure that that advertising will have positive effects and that those ads will make it to the customers.

As it was previously mentioned, maintaining your Facebook page is a very demanding and time-consuming business, especially for smaller companies. Big companies have departments in which people are hired only to maintain and manage the social media accounts of the company and for that job they are well paid. However, smaller businesses do not have such opportunity or funds to employ people whose only task would be to manage social media accounts for that business. In that situation, this task is done by someone else who has different tasks and responsibilities and because of that, those people are not able to fully devote their time to either of their tasks or responsibilities. Besides negative comments or false allegations, people who are dealing with social media accounts, in this case, Facebook, must be available and ready to answer any inquiries or questions about the business because communication on Facebook can convince customers to buy your products or use your services. People expect from pages advertising certain products or services to answers their questions in a relatively short period of time. If this is done in this relatively short period of time, the customer will be satisfied, and that might convince them to buy your products or services. On the other hand, if they do not get their response in a short period of time, they will look for other businesses who will answer their questions relatively quickly and in such way you could lose clients and customers who might even share that information with their circle of friends, whether online or in real life, and in such a way your business might suffer big consequences. Another issue related to this matter is the fact that the Facebook is active 24 hours a day while your business is not. Consequently, questions and inquiries might accumulate on your Facebook page, and it is necessary to answer them as soon as possible because clients or customers will not wait a long time to receive an answer from your business. It is also important not to neglect certain questions or posts no matter how irrelevant or small they might appear.

Since Facebook is a global phenomenon with billion users the competition for attention on Facebook is enormous. In that situation, every business or company is struggling to reach a big number of people. In order to do so, your Facebook ads and post must capture the attention of Facebook users. In order to do that, those posts and ads need to be innovative, original, user-friendly, short and with a clear message. Another important issue is very important when talking about the competition on Facebook, and that is the timing of your posts and ads. If you post your ads at the same time as many other companies, they might get lost in the sea of ads present on the news feed of the customers. Of course, it is impossible to follow all companies' posts and post at the time when no company is posting. However, a little research online will provide you with the best information regarding the best time for posting ads and in doing so, you will be able to find the best time that suits your business and your clients. It may also happen that sometimes other businesses or companies dealing with the same kind of business as you do use your posts or ads to promote their products and services. In order to avoid that kind of situation make your ads and posts as much specific and related to your business as you can. In such way, you will prevent other businesses and companies of taking your ads and using them for their profit and advertisement.

Another big problem in advertising on Facebook are the fake profiles that appear on Facebook regularly. In order to make their fake profiles as much credible as they can, people with fake profiles will like or subscribe to a huge number of pages among which your business may be one. They would often click on your ads or like your posts and in that way giving you information that the number your ads or posts have reached is big but in reality, they would just go through your ads and posts without even taking the time to read it. In that case, you will receive information that many people saw your ads and it might seem to you that your business is becoming more popular. Unfortunately, there is nothing that you can do to prevent this from happening.

Credibility is also among the most important aspects of the advertising on Facebook. As it as previously mentioned, there is a huge number of business and companies who use Facebook to advertise their services and products. Besides those who really are advertising on Facebook there are those who use this possibility for no real reasons. Occupying the space on the clients' and customers' news feed, these, fake ads, take the opportunity from real companies to reach customers and clients through Facebook ads. It is not easy for common people to distinguish between real and fake ads and posts on Facebook and because of that your ads and posts must be as credible as they can be. Reply to all inquiries from customers, be open to suggestions and critics and pay attention to what people want and in that way your ads will distinguish from the fake ones. As we have seen from the previous part, there are a lot of problems when dealing with the advertising on Facebook. Although it may seem that sometimes there is no point of advertising on Facebook, be sure that despite all of these problems, advertising on Facebook is today one of the most popular and the most effective way of advertising. With pretty cheap advertising prices, Facebook is a great platform for businesses to reach wider audiences and find new clients and customers which would be almost impossible without advertising on Facebook. It is important to emphasize that Facebook offers options for all kind of businesses to be advertised on its page. If you are still considering whether or not to use the advertising on Facebook, you must know that in recent years, businesses companies who advertise on Facebook are witnessing increased profits in comparison to the period when they were not using advertising on Facebook. Be sure to check out the experiences of businesses that incorporated Facebook advertising into their marketing strategies in order to experience firsthand the benefits of such type of advertising.

Chapter 4
Twitter

Twitter is an excellent social media marketing tool because it is inexpensive, it is a fantastic way to connect with people and other businesses, is an effective way to build brand awareness, provide your listeners with valuable information, and spy on other businesses. You can learn a lot from other businesses. Pay close attention to industry-specific headlines, your competitors and what your customers are saying. Without fully copying what other businesses are doing, you can see what type of tweets or ads customers are engaging in, and can learn from them before you start your own marketing strategy.

Twitter is particularly important for managing your online reputation, customer service, offering promotions and discounts, and promoting your business. In fact, 60% of people bought from a small or medium-sized business did so because of Twitter. Visual cues on Twitter are a huge selling factor due to the fact that you are limited to 140 characters, and visualization is helpful to add to any tweet. We are also conditioned to pay attention to aesthetically pleasing photos, drawing more attention to a tweet if it is accompanied by a beautiful or intriguing image.

Your Twitter Account Setup

Your Twitter page will show the entire world who you are and what you represent. Therefore, everything you post should accurately reflect you. There are five main parts of your Twitter Page:

(1) Twitter @username – Your username is your Twitter handle. Your handle is what identifies you on Twitter. You have 15 characters. Select something that is identifiable to your business, so either pick the same or something similar to your business name.

(2) Profile Picture – Your profile picture should represent your business, probably a business logo. Something that is very identifiable.

(3) Bio – Your bio allows you to tell people who you are, what makes you who you are, why they should follow you, what you have to offer, any important information about your business such as your contact information, website URL, etc. You only have 160 characters so make it count.

(4) Header Photo – Your header photo is a virtual billboard if you will. You this to display feature products, services, events, promotions, etc. This graphic should often be changed to reflect the most important aspect of your business at the time. Your header photo is a spotlight location!

(5) Pinned Tweet – Your pinned tweet is an important tweet that you want to be pinned at the top of your profile. This should be used to display your latest

news, product developments, discounts or promotions, or upcoming events.

Once you have successfully created your account and have your page setup, you can begin connecting with people and other businesses.

Types of Marketing Content for Twitter

1. Simple Text

Twitter requires all tweets be 140 characters or shorter. Text is common, especially in tweets, RTs (retweets), replies (@replies), and mentions (@mentions).Most text tweets include interesting facts, tips, inspirational or motivating quotes, or asks for RTs. Most text-based tweets do contain a link to some other website. It is also important to note that text tweets are by far the most used tweets.

2. Photos

Just like with Facebook, photos are much more efficient at grabbing someone's attention. Color is the significance here. Color helps people retain information longer and increases a reader's attention span. Photos are perfect on Twitter with the amount of information on a user's feed. Sometimes, when you scroll through Twitter, there is so much information coming at you so fast in tiny bursts of 140 characters. If information is posted with a different type of medium, such as a photo, people will be more likely to stop and check out the information, rather than seeing just plain text, much like the rest of the tweets out there that are flying by. Post a photo of your products, with simple, unique text. You need to be creative to find ways to incorporate your brand into fun photos. All types of photos get shared on Twitter, but humor gets the most shares.

3. Videos

Videos are quite useful when used correctly, but they need to be short and simple. Use videos to give a glimpse into your team, how to use your products, a behind the scene look at your business, or some other informative piece of information that people will find value in. You can even post snippets of a longer video onto Twitter and send people back to your website or your YouTube channel to learn more, incorporating your social media platforms into one another.

4. Slideshares

Slideshares are always good, especially for providing informative and educational pieces of information. These are good for establishing yourself as a leader in an industry. Create one of these instead of writing a blog entry for example. Lessons learned, how-to's, industry information, etc. They're a great way to engage with your followers and allow them to click through at their own pace. If one part is not interesting to them, they can easily skip to the next slide without having to wait it out in a video and get frustrated or lose interest. This also allows you to use photos with text, opening up a broader spectrum of blogging.

5. News Summaries

Twitter allows news organizations and business owners to tweet expanded tweets. The tweet expands allowing you to see an enlarged view of the content and the link provided. You can see a preview of the headline, an introduction and then can continue to the external website to read the rest of the article. It is always good to share current events with your followers, but you can also use this feature for your business. This will also hook people into your blog, newsroom, or article more than a standard text tweet will. By seeing a little bit more of the content and the actual headline, people will be more enthused to click the link and head to the corresponding website.

6. Links

Lots of people tweet with links, but remember to keep it short, use hashtags when possible and make it clear what you want the user to do. If you want them to visit your website, tell them so. If you want them to follow you, tell them that. Be specific and up front. Twitter is not the place to be coy and give long-winded paragraphs of information. Simply tweet for them to visit the link to your website below to learn more about a new product. Include a picture of the product, or whatever you want them to view once at the website, for an added hook on your linked tweet.

Building your Twitter Following

Building your Twitter following is important if you want to maximize your business growth potential and build credibility for your brand. The first thing you need to remember about Twitter is that having a lot of followers does not necessarily mean you are engaging anyone. The only ones who are allowed to have hundreds of thousands of twitter followers without proper engagement are celebrities. People will follow them no matter what, even if they're just tweeting about what they ate for breakfast. You need to make sure you are engaging people so that they share your tweets and are interested in your business.

Think of your tweets as tiny ads for your business. Twitter is like one of your employees who is great at spreading the word about your business. So, first, make sure you are targeted in what you post. By this, I mean do not post too broad. Have a theme and stick to it until you think you can expand. Focus on your business products and services, retweet and share relevant information, post photos of your products, ask your followers to follow you, poll them to find out what they like. The point is, do not jump onto Twitter and start connecting with just anyone. You must engage with people that want to engage. If you're only tweeting a few times a week, that's fine; you do not have to worry. Start small, then slowly work your way up to be more involved with the Twitterverse and get to know your clients and potential clients through

Twitter, letting them get to know you and your business.

Next, you may want to co-market with a fellow business. Run some contests together and offer to give a product away, guest post on their behalf or feature products for each other. The more you do for them, they more they will do for you. Social media is all about networking and connecting with other like-minded individuals. Many businesses would be happy to pair up with you and your business, giving themselves added exposure. Give it a shot, reach out to fellow business owners. It can't hurt; it can only help your reach and engagement opportunities.

Third, engage and engage all the time! It is important that you do your best to have conversations with your followers. You should respond to tweets, take time to share, put energy into communicating and having a relationship with your followers. People like validation and reassurance, so take the time to give them that. Let them know you are there. Let them know that you care they are following you, and you appreciate them. It will only entice more followers. You may forget to respond to tweets in the beginning of your new social marketing campaigns, but that's okay. Do not start fretting and stress yourself out about social media and giving yourself a bad name. Instead, work towards constantly replying to tweets, and then add on sharing, more tweets and more replies. Eventually, you will get to where you need to be. It'll take time to get used to, especially if you're not social media savvy, or do not use it much in your own personal life.

Fourth, promote across your various social media platforms. If you are having a contest on your Facebook page, post it on your Twitter page. There is nothing better than expanding the view of those contests and promotions. Your engagement is sure to grow the more platforms you promote on.

Last, but not least, just be you. Advertise your business based on the marketing strategy you have built and do not veer off unless you see that it is drastically not working. Show the love for your business in your way. The more you make your statement, the more you make a name for your brand. Remember these things: informative, interesting, interactive, personable, and promotional.Below are a few examples of how to get a few more retweets. Try some of these out after you get established in the Twitter world. These will also boost your engagement rates.

"Show your product pride" tweet: RT if you have ____.

"Show you want it tweet": RT if you want to go to ____.

"Interesting fact" tweet: #DidYouKnow That the first hashtag (#) was proposed by Chris Messina?

Quote tweet: Alone we can do so little; together we can do so much. – Helen Keller #quote

Poll tweet: RT if you are single, Favorite if you are not.

The "show your support" tweet: Happy birthday @TonyRomo!! RT to wish him a Happy Birthday!!

The "exclusive content / behind the scenes" tweet: Check out some behind the scenes photos from the "#OneMoreNight video shoot!! – picture of Maroon 5

Tools and Features

Advertising

Twitter allows you to create ads for a particular audience that encourages them to take an action. With any of these campaigns, you can target via account type, device type, behavior, keywords, geographic location, language, gender, interests and more. It is always best to focus on one audience target per campaign for more meaningful insights reporting. Twitter has four basic campaign designs:

Build an audience: By building your audience, you are increasing the number of people that will see your tweets, buy from you, and stay updated on your latest products and events.Website traffic and sales: This ad campaign increases the number of people that will visit your website from Twitter. This campaign is a way to reach more people, increase online sales, and connect with more people.

Promote your app: Promoting your app allows more people to see that you have a mobile app and download it directly from your tweet. Again, you can target your audience and build more engagement.Brand awareness: Promoting your content is one of the most prominent campaigns because you can engage with a larger community of people or a select group of people. You can get your best work in front of the people you want so that they will retweet, reply, and like more of your content.

Twitter Polls

Twitter Polls are a fun way to get followers to engage with you. The poll can have two choice options and can remain open for up from a minimum of five minutes to a maximum of seven days.Twitter Polls are a fun way to learn more about your follower community. Which product is their favorite, which one would they like to see an enhancement to, which color do they like best? This is also a great way to engage with your Twitter community and to get great feedback on your products. If there's something wrong with one of your products and it can be fixed, you will find out! It is also a good way to gauge your reach. Ask your followers if they heard about your event or promotion. There are a lot of ways you can learn more about your followers by using Twitter Polls. Take advantage!

Promoted Tweets

Promoted Tweets are regular tweets that only show to a targeted audience set by you. They do not actually show up on your follower's timeline. They act like a normal tweet, but only show up for those that are in your audience. Those users can react to the tweet, just like it is a normal tweet with likes, replies, Retweets, etc. You can set these up through your advertising campaign or through Twitter Ads. This might be a great idea to use if you have a set audience for one part of your business and another for a different part of your business. If one audience will be using your product, and another wouldn't at all, why would you waste your time, energy and money on the audience that would never buy your product? Quick Promote allows you to promote your best-performed Tweets at any time. If you have a tweet that is proving to be highly engaging, why not promote it to a larger audience? Quick Promote allows you to promote those tweets to larger audiences.

Hashtags: How to Use Them

Hashtags seem simple to use, but when it comes to marketing, likes, and followers, there are a few rules to follow. First, make sure you're using relevant hashtags. They're used to group all tweets that have this hashtag and are of similar content together. If you're promoting boats, using a hashtag regarding boats, or simply #boats will group this with other like-minded people. Second, make sure that they mean what you think they mean. By that, I mean search out the hashtag that you will be using. Are people using the hashtag for things similar to your products, business, etc., or are they using it in regards to something else completely? You do not want your tweets to be falling into categories that just do not make sense. You can use your hashtag in any part of your tweet. It doesn't have to be solely at the end like a lot of users do. Third, do not use these too much. If you find it annoying as a user to see so many hashtags lining up after any post, you find online; others will too. You do not want others thinking of your company in the way that you're thinking about their terrible tweet. Fifth, do not go to great lengths in your hashtags. Keep them short and simple and easy to understand. Keep the long, inside joke type of hashtag for your own personal tweets. Hashtags can be fun, and can help bring more followers to your business if you use them correctly. Follow those simple rules and use accordingly.

Twitter Analytics

Every business owner should be using Twitter analytics to understand how their content is being responded to. Your analytics page is broken down into three main pages: Home, Tweet Activity Dashboard, and Audience Insights Dashboard. Your homepage gives you general statistics from a month-to-month look with a look at your top performing tweets and the influencers in your network. You will see your tweet volume, profile visits, the number of mentions, the number of followers, your top mention, top follower, top tweet, top Twitter, Card, etc. You can easily see what your success has been from this page and who you tend to connect with and engage with the most.

Your Tweet activity dashboard provides with metrics of every single one of your tweets. You will know how many people saw your tweet, liked it, replied to it and Retweeted it. You will gain an understanding of the number of impressions, number of engagements, and your engagement rates for your tweets. You will get detailed analytics as to average per day engagements, profile clicks, link clicks, video views, etc. This is highly effective for helping your marketing strategy. Your audience insights board contains information about your followers. You will get to see how well your follower trend has improved over time as well as learn more about them. You can see more about their interests, demographics, language, geographic location, and gender, device type, behaviors, etc. This information will also lend to helping with your marketing strategy.

Problems with Twitter advertising

Just like Facebook, Twitters offers a number of possibilities for businesses and companies to advertise their products and services. On the other hand, Twitter also displays certain issues that can affect the marketing strategies of your business or companies. The following part will deal with those kind of issues and it attempt to provide solutions for certain kinds of problem that often occur.

One of the most obvious problems that you might encounter while using Twitter for advertising is the limitation on the number of characters that sometimes can be crucial in transferring your message to the clients and customers. Sometimes, it is difficult to say a lot in 140 characters. This is especially the case with businesses and companies who are use Twitter as their basis for marketing strategies. Often, this space is not enough to provide customers with all information they seek in regards to certain product or service. This gets even harder when you want to share a link in your tweet because the link occupies characters and the remaining characters are not enough for you to explain your message. Due to this limitation, tweets often contain vague information that is not enough to evoke interested among the followers and because of that it might seem that your marketing strategy is not working as you intended. Because of this, it may happen that the interaction between the Twitter account of your business or your company gets reduced to a minimum. Your followers must have a reason to click on your tweet and open the link you shared in your tweet. In order for them to open the link, you shared a message that accompanies the link must be attention grabbing. Otherwise, your message will remain unseen.

Just like any other account of social media, Twitter account can be hacked as well. The hacked Twitter account can undo all the good that came out of the Twitter-based marketing strategy in a short period of time. Through only several tweets not written by you but rather by hackers, they can make a negative image about your business or your company that can seem impossible to overcome. Although some people may even say that negative talk is also a commercial for the company, anyone who is serious about their business knows that negative image of a business or a company is often hard to get rid off. While some hackers will hack your account just to prove their ability to do so, others will do it because they might have something against you or your business. In order to avoid this, your account must use all the protection that is available for the profiles of Twitter. Besides that, your password must not be easily detectable, and you definitely should not share the password of your account with anyone outside of the circle of your closest friends and colleagues.

One thing that you need to be especially careful about is the hashtag campaigns that you start. Although you might start these kinds of campaigns in order to promote your products or your services, sometimes these hashtags can backfire and cause more damages that goods. Since people mostly use Twitter for leisure, they would gladly accept a trend of using a hashtag created by certain business or company in order to make fun of that business or company or to point out negative things about the business or company. These kinds of hashtags often quickly become a global phenomenon and as such, they carry a message about your business or your company that you would rather forget. It is often the case that TV news stations pick up the stories about the popularity of certain hashtags especially if they are backfiring to businesses or companies that created them. As a result of TV news coverage of such issues, the number of people who get the negative image of your company is exponentially increased. In order to avoid such situations be careful what kind of hashtag campaigns your twitter account is creating. Check all the facts and make sure that people cannot turn that kind of campaign against your business or your company. With all the negative media attention all the good that your marketing department has done can be undone by one second of bad judgment or bad decision making.

If your business or company has a department dealing with public relations or social media marketing make sure that those people are adequately trained and educated for their job. Otherwise, wrong people in certain positions can result in devastating consequences for your company or your business. In the case when a mad customer expresses his or her anger on your Twitter account you would want for the persons who is going to reply to such message to be calm and to provoke additional conflict with such customers. Otherwise, this also may lead to media coverage and bad publicity for your company. Employees in these departments must be aware that the Twitter account that they are managing is not a personal account and the expression of personal opinions is not acceptable on official accounts of the company. It often happens, that people managing Twitter accounts forget this fact and start to argue and express a personal opinion on certain things and because of the fact that the statement appeared on the companies' twitter accounts it is considered to be the official opinion of that given company. Too often we hear about the bad decisions made by people who misused the companies' twitter accounts and one thing they had in common was the fact that the people managing official Twitter accounts started to express their personal opinions through the official account. This does not happen exclusively on Twitter. All other social networks are also subjects to misuse by people who are managing those accounts.

One of the most common problems in regard to marketing strategies based on Twitter are spams and computer viruses that often accompany a big number of tweets. During the interaction between you and someone who seems to be the customer on Twitter, it might happen that the customer provides certain links for you to open. It often happens that these links are actually computer viruses that infect your computer or your network of computers immediately after you have opened those links. Sometimes, these computer viruses will hijack your Twitter account, and they will demand you to pay a certain amount of money if you want to regain the control over your Twitter account. Besides that, these kinds of computer viruses can create a lot of damage because they can cause damage to your computer to a degree when they cannot be fixed, and you have to buy new equipment. Some computer viruses are programmed to steal your account information after you open the links and when that happens you are not able to control your account anymore. In order to prevent this from happening make sure that your IT department has done an adequate job of providing good anti-virus protection for your computer and make sure that you do not open link that seems suspicious to you or that are coming from the obvious fake profiles. Related to this issues are also spam messages that often arrive on your Twitter account. These types of messages often offer ways to get rich very quickly but in reality, they serve the purpose of infecting your computers with viruses or are created for the purpose of stealing your information after you open that kind of messages.

Often managing of official Twitter accounts of your business or your company can be time consuming which resulted in people being in charge only for managing the social media accounts. Just like with Facebook ads and posts, it is very important to follow the tweets directed at your company. In that way, you will get a feedback information about your products and services because people are willing to share their thoughts with other people on Twitter.

Today, when the social media are the crucial platform for so many important things, people are using Twitter as a way of directly communicating with companies which was almost impossible in the past. When they send a question they expect an answer and if the company does not answer their question they will have a negative image of that company which will only spread among people. In order to avoid that make sure to go through as much of tweets and messages as you or your employees can because sometimes only one response to a certain tweet can prove to be crucial in the general atmosphere in which your business or your company is existing. Make sure to follow the suggestions and critics of your customers on Twitter because companies who accept suggestions and critics are often perceived as good companies. This kind of action will prove to customers that your business or your company is caring for its customers and that is respects the wishes and attitudes of its customers or clients.

One disadvantage of advertising on Twitter is the lack of opportunity to post videos on your accounts. Videos or video messages directed towards the customers or clients are often considered to be one of the best ways of advertising. However, Twitter does not offer a possibility to do that. What you can do is to share the links to those videos. The problem with that is that people rarely open links provided in the tweets due to the lack of their interest or they are afraid that those links are actually computer viruses that can harm their computers. Just like it is a case with Facebook, fake profiles are also a big issue with Twitter as well. Fake profiles that often interact with official accounts of certain businesses or companies often do that in order to do damage to that company because they were damaged by that company or just because they do not have anything better to do. Negative comments are part of online marketing, and you must be ready to deal with such issues because it will play an important role in people construction a positive or negative image about your business or your company.

Some of these issues may be the reason why Twitter is not as much as popular as Facebook in regards to advertising on social media. Some of these issues are can cause serious concerns for people and as such, they create a bad environment for constructing successful marketing campaign. With 340 millions of tweets a day it is easy for your tweet to be quickly forgotten or not even seen and because of that, you need to able to be original and innovative in your approach to the advertising on Twitter. People who are in charge of social media account need to differentiate between official accounts of the company and private accounts because if they do not do that, it might happen that personal opinions are often considered to be the official opinions and attitudes of the company. Not being able to respond to the demands and inquiries of the customers on Twitter will make your company or your business look bad and if that gets picked up by media coverage, it can only result in bad publicity.

Because of that, make sure to spend the necessary amount of time on reviewing the tweets and answering those that need to be answered. This part of the book introduced you to certain issues that often occur when dealing with advertising on Twitter. More importantly, this part tried to provide you with suggestions and solution that can improve your experience of advertising on Twitter.

Chapter 5
Instagram

Instagram is a photo-sharing platform that also allows you to post videos of up to 60 seconds long. Instagram is important because it has over 400 million active users. This is a large audience that you cannot deny engaging with. In fact, Instagram users generally have a larger engagement rate than those on Facebook and Twitter, which is why you cannot look past Instagram. Instagram is shaping up to be the next Facebook, allowing you to actually link your two accounts together (including Twitter and many other platforms as well) instead of having to post on each social media platform. A lot of users are choosing to post only on Instagram, but still have their photos uploaded to Facebook.

Instagram is a lot more personal in the way that Facebook used to be with lots of photos and lots of insight into your own world. Instagram attracts a lot of younger followers, while still branching out to the entire community. While their parents and even grandparents would have a Facebook account, not everyone will have an Instagram account. You can think of Instagram as a great tool to use to engage with a younger audience, staying connected with those you wouldn't necessarily get with Facebook. People like looking at pretty things, so it's no wonder that

Instagram has been doing as well as it has been. The major difference between Instagram and other social media platforms is that you are only posting photos and videos. Your marketing strategy has to be different and well thought-out. You must be creative, visually inspiring and efficient in communication to tell your story.

Your Business Instagram Account Setup

Instagram allows you to create your Instagram account with your Facebook account. I recommend that you do not do that. Instead, use your email address to setup your account so that the two social media platforms are set up separately.As you set up your account, make sure you choose a recognizable name that fits with your brand identity. Your business name or something similar to that so that your customers can find you.

Your profile picture is just as important. It is the thumbnail that everyone will see. It should be your business logo or something that is also recognizable and identifies you as your business (again do not import this image from Facebook as it will ask you if you want to).Your profile basics will be set up next. Put in your business name and a phone number (primary business phone number that customers can use). After that, you can start finding people to follow. My suggestion is to wait until you have your profile and page fully integrated. So, for now, skip this step. Now you can complete your profile adding your website and bio fields. For your bio fields make sure you include who your business is, what you do, where you are located, etc.

The last thing you have to do is set up your social sharing. Now you can link your Twitter and Facebook accounts. It is best to do it here because you can always unlink them. They never HAVE to be tied together. Once they are linked, you can share your Instagram posts to those social media platforms seamlessly. This is a great idea, saving you time and money in having to post to each platform separately, for the same photo or event update.

At this point, you can start posting. I suggest you get a few posts under your belt and make sure you fully understand the new app before you start connecting with others so that you can communicate with them. If you do not like an image or have uploaded one that you thought looked better than it does once you scroll through, you can delete this without many people seeing it. Remember to use hashtags like Twitter to engage with users and find new likes and followers. It is a fairly simple app, so go have fun with it and get to work on your marketing campaign.

Marketing Content for Instagram

As we discussed above, photos and video are the focal points on Instagram. Before you start posting any photo or video, sit down and think about your objective and create a strategy. There are a few things you need to ask yourself to understand truly what direction you want to go on Instagram.

What makes Instagram different? What can you do differently on this platform that you cannot do on other platforms? Who is your target audience and which of those people are on Instagram?

How can you integrate Instagram into your other social media platforms such as Facebook and Twitter? The essence of Instagram is to capture moments, share your unique business culture, show off your products and services, introduce and showcase your team, increase brand awareness, incentive customer engagement, share your events, share news about your business, and connect with other influences.

To do all of these things you need to develop an eye-catching theme that fits with your business and delivers it on a consistent basis. Determine what aspects of your business you are willing to share based on the ideas shared above. Perhaps you have a really beautiful storefront and want to showcase it. Perhaps you and your business are really great at giving back to the community, or are heavily involved in the community. You could post photos of your store (bringing in more recognition to those who may pass by it), or of other storefronts and parks around you. Once you know what subjects you want to share with your audience, brainstorm and determine how you can do that. From there decide if video or photo is best for each objective. Focus on being creative, unique and insightful. There are several apps that you can use to help create the right photo or video. Use these to your advantage to get the right message to your followers.

Establish a content calendar so that you know how often you are going to post, what you will post, what themes you will use, etc. Make sure you set updates for key campaigns and events because this will help you as you develop content. You will have a timeline of due dates and know when photos and videos need to go live. Of course, you can always be spontaneous if something fun or exceptional happens. Spontaneity is a key look to your followers that you're more than just a business. Posting something every so often, at a different time of day, is a great way to keep your Instagram account alittle more personal. The schedule is there to keep you honest and engaged with your followers. However, if you're out with your employees from work or are celebrating something, definitely post this to Instagram. People love to see the inner-workings of a business and showing them the lighter side and your achievements will have people engaging.

It is also best to have some guidelines for what you are going to post. Your overarching style and brand image. Make sure you keep these in mind as you go through this process and that your team understands this. Will you be posting certain things on certain days as a 'feature' or will you only be posting products and product tips? Map out a game plan before you start posting so as not to just jump right into cold and rocky waters. You want to come out strong, engaging fellow

Instagrammers. You want to be consistent so that your followers can easily spot your advertising.

Building your Instagram Following

Hashtags are critical on Instagram. Everyone uses them, but what do they actually do? Hashtags are used to link related content with each other. When you click on a hashtag, a search engine is run, and a list of all relevant content is brought up. The reason you want to use hashtags is because it will enable you to increase your engagement following. Choosing specific hashtags will allow you to connect with others that are using similar tags. Take a look at which hashtags are performing better than others, and stick to those ones. Make sure that they convey the same meaning you intend them to, and that they are relevant to your post.

All major social media platforms use hashtags, with the exception of LinkedIn. Twitter is also very prominent in the hashtag world. Although I did not mention hashtags in my Twitter chapter, Twitter is notorious for hashtags. In fact, the first hashtag was created by Twitter for groups.

Your hashtags need to be specific, relevant and unique. Do not post a photo with 30 hashtags, annoying your followers, or a hashtag that is far too long. Save the last one for your own personal posts that can be construed as a joke to your own followers. There are several hashtags that get used frequently. Some of the top used hashtags are:

#love

#instagood

#me

#follow

#tbt

#cute

#like

#photooftheday

#tagsforlikes

#happy

#picoftheday

#instadaily

#selfie

#friends

Using the correct hashtag for your photos or videos is a hard thing to learn. You need to remember that getting an increase in followers is different than getting an increase in engaged followers. Those are the ones that will increase sales. Do not use hashtags for the sake of getting more likes and followers. Use the above tips in the Twitter chapter with using hashtags on Instagram. Tag your photos and videos properly so that you do get relevant followers. There are apps out there that can help you find the right hashtags. Take advantage of these until you learn what hashtags are correct. Two of the most popular are IconoSquare and Webstagram.

Filters

Strangely, filters are essential to getting a response on your posts.Certain filters are highly popular on Instagram. These filters will increase your engagement. It seems that Mayfair, No Filter, Lo-fi, and Rise are the most popular for increasing engagement. However, for getting more likes and comments, X-Pro II, No Filter, Valencia and Rise are the most popular filters. Try posting with different filters and see what kind of response you get.Using the hashtag 'no filter' (#nofilter) can get you more likes and followers, as there are tons of posts with this hashtag already, and is always growing. Try using it with something that is naturally beautiful, such as an outside shot of your store or warehouse with a great sunset.

Once you get the hang of that particular one, keep going and try out other different filters. Using hashtags and filters together, in a correct manner, will help make your account look more desirable to outside followers. Filters can also help with photos that would be great content, but needs a little photoshopping. Using the filter Clarendon is a great way to brighten your photos, especially of those with nature or buildings, making your post more attractive to viewers. To soften features, with simultaneously brightening the right colors in your photo, use the filter Lark. This filter will make your post look the most similar to your original photo, without taking away, or adding, too many extra colors. Rise will also do the same, giving a softening feature that works wonders on selfies.

Posting Time Table

The timing of your post almost always has an effect on your performance. It is a good idea to run some analysis on your post to see what is working for you. The afternoons seem to be the perfect time to post. Most people appear to sneak a peek at their phones and tablets during the lunch hour and certainly spend some time on their social media profiles after work. The afternoon is a good opportunity to start posting and then use some analysis to determine if there is another time that might be more beneficial.

Another great time to post your photos is first thing in the morning right before 9:00am. People will be just arriving to work, or have already put in a few minutes, but are not yet ready to sit down and do actual work. They'll be having their coffee, maybe some late breakfast and will scroll through their phone while their computer starts up and they can get to work. If putting up a post at certain hours of the day is not working for you and your schedule, there are lots of great programs that can help you set this up, freeing you to log your posts for a week ahead of time, posting it at whatever date you prefer, letting your users think you're posting in real time. This tool is great to use for holidays, letting you stay engaged with your Instagram following while relaxing away from the office.

Tools and Features

Instagram Ad Solutions

Instagram offers an Ads Solution to business owners to help them create and target followers. Their service includes creating the ads through Facebook applications: Ads Manager and Power Editor. Both are excellent applications with themes and content creators to help you create the perfect campaign. You can create photo ads, video ads, or carousel ads. Carousel ads allow you to add multiple photos to the ad so that users can swipe through additional messages. To learn more about designs and getting the results you want visit the Facebook ads guide.

Instagram ads can also include call-to-action buttons. The call-to-actions buttons include clicks to the website, website conversions, mobile app installs, mobile app engagement video views, reach and frequency, page post engagement and mass awareness. All of these are ways to get a user to do something whether it is to promote your website, engage with your ad, drive awareness, download an app, shop, or to simply get more activity.Right now, you can use any Facebook targeting options on your Instagram account. You will need to read and learn about Instagram's Facebook Marketing API to get the most out of your experience.The solution also provides you with analytics so that you understand the performance of your ads and what campaign is the right campaign for you and your business.

Instagram Direct

This is a great tool to use when you want to directly message one of your followers or if one wants to message you. When you put out any contests, events, promotions, or even new hires, asking the users to direct message you are a great way to get personal engagement on Instagram. Instead of chatting through comments, you can have a real conversation that can help you connect with the user better than an impersonal post could. You can send other photos of products, along with a link to your website and set up appointments with direct messaging. Treat this tool as your own real-time chat box for any issues or concerns that may come up with your customers and/or followers.

Problems with Instagram advertising

With Instagram being owned by Facebook you would expect the similar conditions for advertising on Instagram as it is the case with Facebook. However, once you decide to advertise on Instagram, you will notice that this experience is quite different and more problematic on Instagram than on Facebook. One of the biggest problems with advertising on Instagram is the fact is that Instagram does not provide you with the opportunity to target specific groups of people with your ads. Although Instagram is owned by

Facebook and despite Facebook collecting all sort of data from its users, Instagram does not collect almost any kind of data and because of that, it is not possible to single out one group to target by adverts. Consequently, many responses on your ads that you get from Instagram users are in the majority of cases by people who do not at all fit into your group that you targeted at the beginning of the campaign. All of this leads us to a conclusion that often advertising on Instagram can result in losing money because you pay for ads that are not able to reach the targeted group of people. Without the possibility of reaching the group of people for which your product or your service is intended there is almost no point in advertising and it will rarely end up in profit for you and your company.

An additional problem with advertising on Instagram is related to the fact the Instagram application is only available for two operating systems: iOS and Android. This limits the number of people who are able to use Instagram. Consequently, the number of people available for you to advertise to is also limited. However, Microsoft has also provided their users with the Instagram app which little increase the number of people using Instagram. With such limited access, Instagram is not one of the most used social networks for advertising. Although the number of people using Instagram is not small, it is significantly smaller than the number of people using Facebook or Twitter. In comparison to Facebook and Twitter, Instagram until recently has been much more advertising unfriendly. However, recent updates introduced certain options for your businesses or your companies to advertise your products and services. These limits can also reflect on the marketing strategy of your business or your company. Since it might happen that you do not get your money's worth it is realistic to expect that some of you might skip Instagram regarding the advertising on social media.

Since Instagram is a picture sharing application, it is expected of you to provide pictures of your products or your services if you want to advertise on Instagram. This may prove to be difficult since you do not always have the possibility of photographing your product or your service or you are just not able to reduce the service or product on one picture. Although there is a saying that says that a picture is worth a thousand words, this in the case of advertising on Instagram cannot be applied. The picture you take and decide to put on Instagram must reflect all ideas of your business or your company. You want your clients and customers to be able to understand what your company or business stands for. This might get a bit difficult when you have only one picture to do so. Additionally, pictures you post on Instagram must be attractive and attention grabbing for customers and client. Otherwise, your adverts might end up unseen. Original ideas and innovative approaches to picture taking and sharing often lead to the increase in the people's attention for the given picture. So, if you are willing to do advertising on Instagram make sure that you are familiar with the filters and picture editing materials because that will help you to reach a higher number of people through Instagram. Combining the picture, filters and the use of hashtags on Instagram you are able to reach the people but that does not guarantee that they will open or like your picture or follow your account on Instagram. Additionally, one of the problems with advertising on Instagram is related to the text that you can write beneath the picture and can be used for sending a direct message to clients and customers. However, a small number of people actually reads that caption so do not be surprised if you do not get the expected reaction from the ad that you put on Instagram including the message together with the picture.

One of the reasons why people do not read such text is that it often happens that the text following the pictures is too long, and people just do not want to read the long text and because of that they skip such posts and focus on posts that do not require them to do a lot. Consequently, the text that accompanies the pictures you put on Instagram needs to be short, clear, well written, organized and user-friendly in order for the Instagram users to pay any attention to it. Otherwise, your money will be spent in vain. In order to be present on Instagram and among the popular accounts, you need to post a huge number of pictures because more pictures you post the possibility of reaching a wider number of people is greater. However, this takes up a lot of time. Because of that, some companies hire people just to manage the Instagram account of their companies because it requires a lot of attention and time. If you do not post pictures often on your account, your followers will most likely unfollow your profile and follow someone else who regularly publishes pictures. Not publishing pictures on Instagram can result in losing the big number of your clients and your customers because they want to be familiar with the latest things concerning your business or your company. And if you do not give them that possibility it is hard for them to remain interested in your products or your services.

One of the most important issues related to the advertising of Facebook is related to the issue of copyright ownership. Once you put a picture on the Instagram account of your business or your company it is almost impossible to control who shares the pictures and who uses is for their own personal gain. The copyright infringement is a very common occurrence on the social media especially on Instagram because you do not have any tools to prevent people from using your pictures for their own personal purpose. The problem occurs when businesses or companies that deal with the same products or services as you start using your photographs for their marketing campaigns without asking for permission basically hijacking your marketing campaign. The funds that you invested in advertising on Instagram in this case are used to fund someone else's advertising campaign and once other companies start to use your promotional material it is almost impossible to stop them from doing that because there is almost no protection of copyrights when you post pictures on Instagram. This, however, does not happen only Instagram. Every other social media is subject to copyright infringement because there are few instrument on these social media that can actually prevent people from using your marketing campaigns and your marketing ideas for their own personal gain. In order to avoid problems of this kind make sure that your Instagram posts have a watermark or your logo somewhere in the picture. This, however, does not guarantee that others will not use your pictures for their campaigns, but it will definitely make that process a much harder and in some cases it even might prevent them from using such Instagram pictures.

Just like it is the case with every other social media used for advertising purposes, the interaction between your business or your company and the customer on Instagram is of crucial importance. Answering on the comments that your customers, clients or just followers left on your Instagram posts shows to them that you are devoted to your customers and that you pay much attention. Incorporate their ideas, suggestions, and criticism into your marketing strategies in order for your marketing campaigns to be much more effective. When people see that you reply to their comment or their question the image of your company or business immediately receives a positive boost because it shows that you pay attention to what people are actually saying. Reply to those comments, provide additional information about the products or services that people are asking for and be kind and use appropriate language, and your marketing campaigns will witness enormous increase your business' or your company's popularity. Not only will your business or your company be characterized as customer friendly and customer oriented, but the positive talk about the company will also ensure a bigger number of clients and customers for your company. As in many other aspects of our lives, being kind really pays off. On the other hand, one misjudged answer to provoking comment can result in a negative campaign against your business or your company. In order to avoid that make sure that people who manage your business accounts know what they are doing and make sure that they know the difference between the private and official Instagram account.

Just like on every other social media, it is impossible to measure the people's reaction to what you are posting on Instagram. Because of that, it is impossible to know how many people actually opened your posts and interacted with it. Because of that some business owners actually wonder is there a point of investing money and time into this kind of advertising campaigns because they are not able to measure the impact those campaigns have to their clients or on their customers. Since a huge majority of business owners want to see the results of marketing campaigns as soon as possible, the marketing campaigns on social media may seem to them a waste of time because they have to wait a certain period of time to notice the first results of that type of campaign. With this in mind, they often neglect or fail to see the benefits of this kind of advertising campaign. Since social media are global phenomenon a little is required for your product or service to become widely popular and when that happens you will see that the benefits for your business or your company can only be achieved through this kind of marketing campaign and that no other marketing campaigns offer them the possibility of directly interacting with their clients or customers. To a certain extent, in connection with this aspect is the feedback that you get from your followers. This feedback is in the majority of cases a positive with people positively reviewing your products or your services.

However, there is also a negative feedback, and the problem of this feedback is that it is public and that everyone can get involved in discussions even without trying your products or your services. Not being able to control negative feedback is a very big challenge for businesses and companies. When it is handled correctly, this negative feedback can even be used to promote your company but in the majority of cases, this negative feedback results in people obtaining negative pictures about your business and your company. Good management of this kind of feedback ensures the clients and customers that you have heard what they are saying and that you care about what they actually have to say. It is a small effort for you to answer such comments or questions but they serve a much greater purpose that you at your current level might not even recognize.

Once again, the importance of social media advertising campaigns is reflected in this part as well. If you want your company to follow the trends and remain popular, social media advertising campaigns are something that your company must start to use. Instagram advertising campaigns are sometimes hard to manage because it seems hard to reach the targeted group of people. However, with millions and millions of people using Instagram daily, being present on such platforms can only result in benefits for your business or your company. Good management of the Instagram account of your business may prove crucial in obtaining new clients and customers so make sure that people who manage these accounts know what they are doing.

It is important to emphasize that numerous benefits definitely outweigh all the problems and negative things related to marketing campaigns based on Instagram. Although these problems may seem like something not worth of dealing with, you will see that the consequences of missing out on Instagram marketing campaigns have much more bad effects on your company and on your business. Since the social media are the present and the future of marketing campaign, it would be a devastating for your company or your business to miss out on such a great opportunity especially because the cost of advertising on social media is much lower than the cost of standard ways of advertising.

Chapter 6
YouTube

YouTube is not just for posting videos to enhance and grow your career as an artist, celebrity or actor. YouTube has become an effective form of marketing for businesses. Using YouTube is important because you can expand your reach and engagement.One of the benefits of YouTube includes capturing your audience's attention. Using your creative genes to capture more attention can help any business, allowing you to go further with your company's brand. YouTube can be a fresh way to draw in new followers, increase brand loyalty, expand your reach with a relatively low budget, and improve your SEO (search engine optimization).

YouTube has more than one billion users, which means it is one of your best opportunities for marketing and outreach. With that many users, you have the chance to pull in several new potential customers. YouTube is one of the best social media platforms for reaching more people. There are many ways to use YouTube to your advantage, be it ads or your own videos. Embedding YouTube videos is easy, which means you can include these videos on your website and share them on all of your other social media accounts. Viewers can easily share them with their friends and pass them on from there. The ability to share your video makes YouTube a highly successful marketing effort. It is the perfect avenue for sharing your products and services.

You may or may not know that Google owns YouTube. With Google's search engine optimization, YouTube videos are consistently ranked high in search results. The ability to have your videos ranked high means you must utilize this marketing strategy. It is a powerful way to increase your search engine optimization results and increase your online presence. Once you are constantly found at the top, you will be finding more and more customers and leads coming to your business. With this said, YouTube must be included in your marketing strategy. Videos are a highly effective way for users to engage with your content. There are tons of ways that you can get more followers, more leads, and more customers, simply by making videos. You can choose from numerous types of videos to make, choosing only one, or playing with them all and seeing which works the best for you. Shaking it up every once in a while, with a different type of video can help keep your users attentive and is a fun way to get your brand out there and use those creative muscles.

Your YouTube Channel Setup

YouTube does not have business accounts. You will need to register just like everyone else. I do not recommend that you use a personal email address for your set up. Use something that you will be comfortable sharing with others on your team so that other people in your business can help manage the YouTube channel. If using your generic business e-mail is not working for you, create a new e-mail solely for your YouTube (and overall business) ventures. That way, if someone needs to get into the account for any reason, you won't have personal messages (be it business or home-related) out in the open for everyone to see.So, go ahead and click on the button 'Create an account' to register for a new account on the YouTube homepage.

You will be asked for some basic profile information: name, username, password, birthday, phone, and email address. Make sure you select something that reflects the business name as your username. I would recommend the business name or something very similar.After you are done you will be asked to set up a new profile for the Google account, skip this step for now.

Once this is done, YouTube will automatically set up a YouTube channel for you. At the bottom right, you will see the channel set up page. You will see the question: Would you like to appear on YouTube as a different name, brand or organization? With a link next to it that says 'Create a username.' Click this to fill out your business name so that your channel will reflect your business and not you as an individual.Your channel is now officially set up. Below I will talk more in depth about YouTube's Branded Channels features, which gives you more advanced options and design opportunities. At this point, you can go back and update your profile with more business information.

Types of Marketing Content for YouTube

Promotional Videos

Promotional videos are often used by businesses to advertise their brand. They usually include a four-step process – a problem, solution, how the solution works, and a call to action. You want these videos to remain short maybe a minute or two and focus on the benefits of the product. Be entertaining and use music to evoke emotion.There are nine elements of a promotional video that will help you master the video and evoke sales: establish a personal bond, movement, curiosity, irresistible offer, the art of rhetoric, the creation of mass enemy, adding value, call to action, and memorable tagline.

Last, make sure you have a script and have rehearsed it so that the video works. Trying to make a promotional video without rehearsing what you're going to say, and really thinking it through, will end up disastrous. Users will begin not to trust you and your videos, declining their sales in your brand. Remember: you're not making a video 'Prank for your friends, here. You're making a video for your clientele; keep it professional, clean and engaging.

Interviews

Interviews with industry experts are great videos to post on your channel. You can also interview employees, behind-the-scenes footage of your business, event footage, footage of fans, etc. The most important thing to remember is to use real people with real stories. Be genuine and unscripted. If its natural, your audience with form a bond. With that being said, make sure you write out, beforehand, what questions you want to ask the industry expert, employees, etc. A lot of people get camera shy once it's in their face, and can lose track of what they wanted to say. There's a difference between a few 'uh's' and 'um's' in a video making it look natural and relaxed, and completely forgetting what you're going to say next and how to respond.

How-To's and Product Tutorials

Demonstrations of products are great because you get to show your audience what benefits they will get from using your products. You get to put the enthusiasm and fun into the video. You get to show your audience the belief you have in your business and your products. Try making a How-To video that someone who doesn't use your particular product, but a similar one, might want to watch. It may seem counter-intuitive, but by slowly adding videos that can appease the masses, you can gain more subscribers, likes, and leads. Always be informative in your videos, adding humor or flare when needed to wake up an otherwise dry demonstration. To do this properly and to be effective, make sure you do your homework, have a script, keep it short, avoid overloading them with information, and finish with a strong call to action so that they know exactly what to do next.

Presentations

Presentations are typically used to unveil new product lines or new, bigger and better products. These are slightly larger productions than the other videos. These videos need to be big, powerful and change the way your audience will think of your products. You need to think out of the box and be unique. These are your most powerful motivators that will bring in new clients, and strengthen your bond with existing clients. Think of these videos like a presentation at a boardroom table. Those who come in weak, stumbling and mumbling won't get a good review and will most likely get passed over for that promotion a few months later. Those who come in strong, knowledgeable, entertaining and engages with those around them will receive great feedback, will be admired and will be thought of when the next promotion comes up. Presentation videos do not have to be boring and dry. You can keep them up-to-date by bringingin new information and entertain your clients and your future clients in one fell swoop if you take your time to research, rehearse and think outside the box.

User Generated Content

User generated content is content that your audience comes up with on their own. You encourage them to produce content by coming up with a hashtag and a contest or something similar. Do something entertaining that encourages your audience to get involved. User generated content is probably the hardest of the marketing content, but probably the most useful. By running this type of campaign and using their ideas, you're showing that you're engaged with your audience and that you respect your customers' opinions. Try asking them what their biggest frustration is with any product or even with a product that your company carries. It may be that the user doesn't know how to use the said product, resulting in another How-To video as well.

If it's something that's actually wrong with one of your products, this is a great time to hear about it, instead of receiving mass complaints that you will have to herald later. This may even bring you three extra videos that will capture your user's attention: The User Engagement video which you can make simply stating that you're working on these issues and will be unveiling a better product soon; the Presentation video that will showcase the product and everything that it does better than its predecessor; and the How-To video that will show the users how to use this new and improved product. You always want to be thinking of ways that each video can correspond with the others, bringing them together in one easy batch that subscribers and other YouTube users can find and use.

YOUTUBE ADVERTISING

Just like on Facebook, Twitter, and Instagram, you can use YouTube as a platform for video ads. What

Social Media

was once the most common place for ads, television, YouTube is taking this over and starting fresh. As each video gains more subscribers, views, and likes, YouTube will place an ad in front of it. Some you may not be able to skip and only run for 20-30 seconds. Others, you can skip at a certain mark (30 seconds). Make a video about your company, stating what you do, what you sell, etc. and take advantage of YouTube advertising. This is your time to be playful and energetic about your company, your goals, products, and values. Opt for your own budget, and how many times your video will appear. You can also target specific audiences, such as age and location, plus many others.

YouTube offers a view-by-ad budget. Anything after the 30-second mark on those videos that you can skip will get billed to you. If your video is under 30 seconds, the viewer has to skip before the end of the video. Anything before is free advertising. Use those minimal seconds to get the most intriguing and entertaining part of your video out. If a video, even if it is solely an advertisement, looks interesting, a user will sit through the advertisement to see what the end game is. A great example is the gathering that comes during the Super Bowl, solely for the commercials. What was once an annoyance and a point in the game to get refreshments is now part of the show.

Use this same kind of thought process for your own YouTube advertisements You can make a Presentation or How-To video for your advertisement instead of making a typical commercial video explaining your company. Make this video more upbeat than your regular How-To videos, with a little more excitement, intrigue, and fun. If this type of video gets great reviews from those watching, try making more How-To videos like your advertisement, bringing in new customers and/or expand your fan base. To keep you looped in with your new audience and numbers, YouTube offers Analytics for your YouTube ads that will help you track if this is the right area of marketing to be spending your money. Always make sure to check your numbers before running another ad. One specific ad set may be performing better than another, so why would you continue to run the one that is not doing as great? If you find a niche that viewers are loving, stick with it! You can always try new ideas and add them in to run beside these working ads to see if any differences pop up. YouTube advertising is a great way to get your name out further than simply making a video or two on your own YouTube channel.

Building your YouTube Channel

YouTube is a hard market for business, but can be one of the best marketing strategies if it is used correctly. Most businesses do not invest in YouTube marketing because it is difficultand can be time-consuming and expensive (if you're using professional videography). However, 17% of all internet traffic is on YouTube and YouTube is the second largest search engine on the worldwide web. So why not use it?There are a few keys to building your YouTube channel following.

First, who are you creating your content for? Who out of your target audience is going to be watching these videos? Obviously, the same as those that will be buying your products. Therefore, your methodology and strategy for creating videos need to be focused on just that. Do not think you are selling to the entire world, because you know every business has a niche market. Focus in on your audience and create your videos for them, not everybody. If you're not getting many views right off the bat, remember that you are selling to a niche market, and this is not a music video or a make-up tutorial, which are frequently searched by users. Keep up your videos, making them more polished and professional as time goes on and your viewers will come.

Second, what is your audience's primary goal What do you have to offer them? What matters to them? What do they need? Once you understand more about what they need and want, you can relate your business to them and/or offer new products based on their needs. Remember, you do not have to focus on the entire audience. You can separate your target audience into groups.To attack more views, make sure you are entertaining or accomplishing a goal. Most people watch videos to be entertained or to learn how to do something or more about something. Establish your goal and make your videos useful from there. Always, always make sure you make quality videos. If your videos are low quality, they will be useless because they will not be watched. If your budget allows, try hiring a videographer for those videos that take precedent, such as your video ads or specific promotional videos. If your budget doesn't allow to hire a videographer and use their equipment, buy a professional-grade camera that you can use to snap photos for your other social media accounts and that will produce videos for your YouTube account. The better the video, the more views and likes you will receive.

Most importantly set up a routine schedule for posting new videos. The more you post, the more you will get subscribers who come back to watch more. Successful marketing is about putting good quality material in front of your audience, so do so regularly.

Tools and Features

Branded Channels

A branded channel on YouTube is a more customizable channel that allows you to customize the appearance of your channel so that it looks more like your website (including banners and background images). It is a better way to promote your business and advertise your brand. Your branded banner can include links to your other social media platforms so that viewers can easily get to your Facebook page, Twitter, and all other accounts. They all integrate very nicely.

You are also given an analytics management page so that you can monitor the performance of your channel including metrics and tracking of viewers. How many visits you get, the best performing videos, worst performing, etc. Analytics will help in creating new content as you grow your channel and learn more about your audience. I've said it many times before, but keeping up with these analytics and tracking every little detail is very imperative. You wouldn't go out and spend thousands of dollars on a new vehicle without making sure that it passes many tests, would you? The same is true when marketing on social media. If you're chucking in hundreds (or thousands) of dollars into one venue and idea and it's not working, re-evaluate your strategy. It may be just the creative content that is not working for viewers, the professional quality (or lack thereof), or it could end up that YouTube is not right for your business. If posting many videos on YouTube turns out to not be rightfor your business, still keep your account and use it to upload videos onto your website or other social media sites. YouTube can essentially be your hub for all marketing videos because you can embed them on your website and other platforms.

Analytics

YouTube comes with an analytics page as most social media accounts do. Most users of YouTube are looking for the analytics of the number of views and likes and how much money they've spent and where. You can also look at where the viewers were finding your video (under which category, if on YouTube itself, or generic search), showing you where to put your next video(s). This will even show you a report for your audience retention, showing you how well viewers stuck it out with your video(s), and letting you compare to other videos with similar content. This is a great tool to use, especially if a lot of videos tend towards the drier side.

People's attention spans have deteriorated over the years, so placing the most intriguing part of your video in the first 15-30 seconds is important. If they're going to stick it out until the end, they're most likely true followers. If you use the first 15-30 seconds of your video (with attention spans waning the closer you get to 30 seconds) to get your brand, product or services out in the open right away, you can still chalk that up to a good marketing video. The more people see your name, the more likely they're going to think of you when it comes time to use your services or product.

Interactive Features

Google allows you add interactive features to your videos using AdWords on your videos. You can use the following interactive features to meet a goal:

Cards: Use cards to increase engagement and brand awareness. You have the ability showcase your new products and/or promote other videos on your channel.Call-to-action Overlays: Creates an action to entice viewers to visit your website.

Shopping Cards: Encourages viewers to view your products and purchase them from your Merchant Center account.

Problems with YouTube advertising

As we have seen from previous parts of this books, even social media marketing strategies are not without its problems and issues that affect the general image that your business or your company has in the world and among your clients and your customers. YouTube with being one of the most popular social media marketing instrument also has certain issues that may prove to be problematic for your company when trying to advertise on this social media.

One of the most important issues of the marketing strategies of YouTube-based marketing strategies refers to the fact that there is no guarantee that your YouTube advertising campaign will be successful. Nothing can guarantee that YouTube viewers who are also your customers will like your ads and your videos and consequently like your business or your company. YouTube users have the possibility of deciding whether they want to see the video or not. Because of that, you have to be able to convince users to click on your link and to watch your video. It can often happen that if your promotional videos on YouTube are not well done or if the YouTube users notice certain problems with your ads they might emphasize that problem in their posts on social media whether it is by commenting on your YouTube video or sharing the link on their Facebook or Twitter page. Either way, negative image of your company is being spread around the social media. Even when the users watch your video, that does not mean that your marketing campaign is showing results. In order for those marketing campaigns to be successful, YouTube users must like and support the video that promotes your products or your services. Otherwise, the YouTube users' rejection will mark the marketing campaign as the failed one and all the intended benefits of such campaigns will have to be put on hold while the campaigns go under reimagining.

Another important issue in regards to YouTube-based marketing strategies is the lack of possibilities for you to make your promotional videos more customer friendly. These limitations imposed by YouTube significantly limit the scope of ads that can be used by companies in attempting to reach a bigger number of people. Besides this, too long promotional videos can cause people to abandon watching your video and in that way not getting the message you intended for them to receive upon watching your promotional videos. Not only that your promotional videos need to be short and on point with the message you are trying to convey, but they also need to be original and innovative. This is because there is a huge number of promotional videos out there and people of tired of watching the same old adverts over and over again. Consequently, they will not watch promotional videos that do not differ in any way from all other videos out there. In order for them to watch your video, it needs to show originality and innovation; to show something that users have not previously seen and to awake their interest for your products or services. Creating a video like this is not an easy job. That is why there are professionals who specialize only in creating YouTube promotional material. It is not enough for the video to have one captivating moment. It needs to be able to capture the attention of the viewers from the very beginning because YouTube users decide in the first couple of second whether or not to finish watching the video they have selected.

Since YouTube is an open platform which means that anybody can upload videos or comment the already uploaded videos it gets hard not to have negative reviews and comments on your promotional material. If they did not like your promotional video on YouTube, those users will show their disappointment in the comment section by badly reviewing not only your promotional video but your company as well. This is not the only case when negative comments or reviews appear. That kind of reviews or comments will often appear randomly without any real reasons because there are people whose only goal is to spam those kinds of videos and to post negative comments and reviews. The problem with these kinds of comments is that they cannot be controlled or deleted, and everybody else is able to see such comments when they open your video. Knowing this, you have to ready for such comments, and you have to have a strategy that will deal with that kind of people and the type of comment they post on your videos. Make sure that people who are managing your YouTube channel are familiar with this type of comment and give them clear instruction of what to respond to such comments and reviews. Provide them with all necessary information need to soften the blow induced by such negative comments because the way you respond to such comments might convince more people that your company or business takes care of not only people who are satisfied with their business but also takes care of those who are not satisfied. Just like with any other marketing strategy, it is also important to incorporate the ideas, suggestions, and criticism provided by your clients and customers into the marketing strategy and into the official business of your company.

Another important issue in relation to YouTube promotional videos is the fact that those videos can be deleted by YouTube itself if the videos do not respect the rules set forth by the YouTube administration. Certain things are not allowed even on the open platform such as YouTube. If the YouTube administrators notice these things in your videos, your videos will be automatically deleted without previous notification. This can prove to be very costly because you can spend a lot of money on creating a video only for that video to be deleted by YouTube because it breaks certain rules. This can be controversial because some things you think are appropriate and important for your business or your company and you want them included in the video, YouTube might think of those same things as inappropriate and might decide to delete them without any previous notification. It might also happen that YouTube administration decides and deletes your YouTube channel completely. This might happen if your videos are constantly breaking the rules and policies of YouTube. If that happens, all your previous video material will be lost, and you will be left without the possibility of reaching people through YouTube videos. In order to avoid these kinds of problems, make sure that you have read and understood all the rules and policies that YouTube has for its users and make sure that your videos do not break any of these rules and policies.

Although YouTube offers a basic analytics tool, it is far from being enough for you to make analyses of the marketing strategies which would later determine the way in which your other marketing strategies will go. Just like Instagram, it is not possible for you to get the adequate information about the demographics or the people that are interested in your videos and consequently in your products and in your services. Marketing strategies are used for gathering information about the customer's wishes and demands as well as promotion of the certain product or service. In this aspects, YouTube promotional strategy does not provide with adequate and required information for your to be able to incorporate that data into your official policies.

Uploading videos on YouTube platform is not enough. You cannot just upload promotional videos to your channel and expect the job to be finish. In some degree, the job is just starting there. Once you upload videos on YouTube, you need to promote that video because if you do not promote a video only a few people will be able to see it. One way of doing that is by paying YouTube to promote your videos. This option seems to be the best solution for th quick promotion of your video, but, on the other hand, it will make you spend a certain amount of money in order to do that so the costs of marketing strategy might even get higher. Another way to promote your videos on YouTube is to share them on your social media accounts. The problem with this type of promotion is that it limits the number of people who can see that post. If you share this video on your Facebook page only people who liked your page and who are following you will be able to see the post. If you share this video on your Twitter account, only people who are following you will be to see your tweet and even then it is questionable whether or not they will click on your link and see the actual video. With all this being said, it is clear that spending additional money on paying YouTube to promote your videos is the best solution because in that way there is no limit regarding the number and the type of people who can see your video.

In the previous parts of this book, we mentioned that there is a possibility of other people hijacking your campaign and turning them to promote them instead of you. This also happens when you do YouTube promotions as well, only slightly a bit different. When you are posting a video on YouTube, you are not able to provide links to your products or services in the name of the video. Instead, you have to come up with the title of the video. When you upload a promotional video and after some time it gains popularity, it might happen that other companies or businesses dealing with the same or similar business as yours upload the videos under the same or slightly different title. This is done because when you open certain videos, the suggestion box will provide you with the link to videos that contain similar title as yours. In giving similar names to their videos, they steal attention from your video and try to make their video more popular. Since there are no copyright guarantees in relation to the names of the videos that you can use when uploading new promotional videos there is nothing that can be done in order to prevent others from stealing the attention and popularity from your videos.

Another issue that can prove to be important for business owners who invest money in creating a video for YouTube promotion and spend money on paying YouTube to actually promote that videos is the fact that occasionally YouTube servers are offline. Consequently, YouTube users are not able to reach that kind of videos which reflects on the popularity of certain business or a company that pays for YouTube promotions. Not being able to access the videos you paid for might seem as wasting money on such projects because when YouTube is offline, there is no point of having promotional videos on such video platform.

As we have seen from this part, even YouTube is not without its problems in regards to marketing strategies of the companies. However, many people think that the future of marketing is actually marketing on YouTube those who decide to turn their attention to promotion on YouTube will be provided by a great opportunity to reach a huge number of people in a very short period of time. Consequently, the results of this kind of marketing strategies can be seen in a very short period of time. The benefits of such advertising are much bigger than the costs of such advertising or marketing strategy. It is important to once again emphasize that your promotional videos need to respect certain rules and policies set forth by the YouTube administration because, otherwise, there is a possibility for your videos to be deleted as well as for your channel to be permanently deleted as well. Besides advertising on Facebook, advertising on YouTube seems to be the best choice if the marketing strategies are focusing on social media advertising.

Chapter 7
LinkedIn

LinkedIn is like a mixer for the internet. This is the place to be if you want to make easy connections and network your way around your industry and beyond. Instead of having to head to stuffy and boring get-togethers designed around networking, all you have to do is find profiles that would fit for your business and beyond, and continue connecting. Accepting connection invitations is easy, and will be coming frequently when you first sign up. The more connections you have, the more you will begin to find and initiate on your own. Try adding your entire address book to your LinkedIn profile and start networking.

Once someone has accepted your invitation to connect, send them an e-mail thanking them for connecting and tell them a little bit more about yourself and your company. You can even ask them if they would like to sign up for any newsletter that you may or may not have at this point in time. If you do not have a newsletter for your company, it's best to get one. This can definitely help you inform your clients beyond social media and ties everything together. Some may like to look at your various platforms and pages, but do not want to go any further. Instead, receiving a newsletter with the most important points laid out easily for them to read or watch is a great way to keep them informed.

Although a great place for employers to check out future or find potential employees, LinkedIn can do more than just find your next great employee. Marketing with LinkedIn is simple and easy to use, benefitting your company greatly. You can even use LinkedIn to generate leads, bringing people back to your website or blog. Use your website and blog posts on your LinkedIn profile, as well as when you are posting in the newsfeed. Also, use your own links when commenting in LinkedIn groups, as well as on any of your showcase pages, which will be discussed on how to use to your potential later on in this chapter. All posts should be geared towards business-minded people. Sure, you can share a few office photos on your profile and videos that are not completely serious but keep those to the minimum. Motivation, business tips, insider tips, and product information is key to marketing yourself on LinkedIn. Statistical updates, business advice, product numbers, and descriptions rule the newsfeed. For a bolder approach, try targeting your posts to specific audiences. As long as you have 100 or more users, you can target your audience for any posts that you put out there on LinkedIn just like you would with a targeted ad campaign.

YOUR LINKEDIN PROFILE SET-UP

Once you've made your company profile, make sure that your employees have their own LinkedIn profiles that you can use as connections. Future employees and clients will be able to see who is working with you and your company, and feel like they get to know you a little better. Having a proper LinkedIn profile is like having your entire resumé out in the open for everyone to see your accomplishments. Make sure that your profile is neat, organized and covers everything that anyone would need to know about your company. Complete all fields, even if they seem mundane and useless. Start with your professional photo. If you do not have specific headshots, get someone to re-create a headshot look with you looking clean and professional. Make a Headline. Use roughly ten words to make a headline that will stand out amongst the crowd. If you have any specialization, this is where you would put it. Summary Field. This is where you can brag about your achievements. Write these down in bullet points in clear and concise wording.

Add images, videos, and documents. Do you have a video about your company? Here is a great place to add it so people can get to know you and your company a little better. Add your work history. If you worked at a fast food restaurant when you were 14, but you're now the CEO of your own company and have worked in many other offices, this is not the place to add in that fast food company. Use your work history to outline why you and your company has gotten this far already. Link your Website. Do you have a website or multiple websites? Add a link to your website in your profile. Use a call-to-action button to spruce it up and make it more inviting for LinkedIn users to click on.

If you're making your company page, simply click on Interests and Companies. You can create your company profile here and should use the above format to fill out every single field that you are able to. Filling out everything in your profile, both your personal and your company's makes it more engaging for those who are looking for new hires, new opportunities and to use your company. People are nosey, and always want to know everything; the more information you have about your professional life that is available to future clients and connections, the better.

TYPES OF MARKETING CONTENT FOR LINKEDIN

There are many different types of marketing strategies with LinkedIn. You can use any of the notes below for mass targeted audiences, or you can streamline your lead generation into something that may take a little bit more time but can produce winning results. LinkedIn is all about networking and introducing yourself to others in your field and abroad, so why not introduce yourself to those who would be most likely to use your product or services? This is the same kind of idea that door-to-door knocking or coldcalling takes on, but a lot easier to do while at home or in between meetings. Keep in touch with those who have seemed to be intrigued by your company, and not bothering those who are not. If people specifically say they do not want to be contacted anymore, this is not an invitation to try again at a later date. This is meant for you to back off and let your web presence and advertising speak for itself They may not be ready to use you now, but they may be down the road. Keep it light if there are any flat-out rejections and move on. Remember: door-to-door knocking doesn't result in every single person signing up – you have to knock on many doors before you even get one signature.

Sponsored Content

This is where you can send direct messages to a specific targeted audience. Here, you can create messages for specific products to go out to only one audience, while another can go out to a different audience. By building your own custom audiences, you can get your messages as personal as need-be, creating a space for new clients and existing clients. You get to create your own budget and have the option to use either pay-per-click or pay-per-impression, depending on what your marketing needs are.

Sponsored InMail

A great way for networking and finding employees, you can set your target audience, and send out messages that would pertain to them. This is a great tool to use if you want to promote your YouTube video tutorials or presentations.

Dynamic Ads

The biggest payoff when putting out ads on social media is that you can target your audience accordingly. Do you want to target a broad audience? A smaller audience? You can find out the company size that would be likely to be buying your product, as well as honing in on the industry that would be most susceptible to buying your product or services. Using advanced targeting can help you get your business off the ground and growing. Using metrics to track your ads and see how well they're performing is a no-brainer for any business to be using. You always want to be tracking your ads and information, because how else would you ever know how your business is faring? If one ad is not working out, you can simply test out and switch to a new one.

Display Ads

Display ads are placed on high-traffic LinkedIn pages, and your budget is worked out by the cost per impression. You can use audience targeting, like normal, even going so far as using third-party data. You can choose from either a 300X250 banner or a 160X600 banner found on the side of the LinkedIn page. These banner sizes are set for those on desktops, only.

Text Ads

Text ads are those smaller ads that you may see popping up with your 'interests.' You can target your audience, of course, and can either send people to your LinkedIn profile or to your website. I would suggest sending them to your website as that's where you're going to want the leads coming from. You should have more information on your website, and more contact information for them to either fill out or call you with. You choose how you pay, either per click or per impression. And, are allowed to add a 50X50 image; if you are going to use a text ad, definitely include with it an image. People are more inclined to click on something if an image is included. Think of it as an online dating profile; people want to see what/whom they are interacting with.

LinkedIn Groups

Joining a group is a great way to meet other like-minded individuals. The same is true when joining a group on LinkedIn. Try and get involved with more than one group, striking off each area that you can benefit from, such as motivation, advice, and information from those in the similar field as yourself; as well, find ones that can be more like your Monday Morning Power Breakfast. There, you will be able to discuss business tips and advice, the same as the other group(s), but you will also be helping each other out with your own product(s) and service(s). Find those groups that would be most likely to use your product(s) or service(s).

Do not be afraid to make your own group. Creating a group can be a little intimidating; you may have the idea that no one will want to join, or others won't find it useful and will leave. However, do try to make one. It's a great way to build your network, your followers, and a great way to find new clients. You'll look like the one 'in the know' in your industry, reaching out to others with similar interests and likes.

BUILDING YOUR CONNECTIONS

You've already invited everyone in your address book, and you've joined some groups and even made one yourself. However, you still want to build your connections and grow your presence on LinkedIn. Now what? The way to get more noticed on LinkedIn is to be continuously out there, showing off your professional attributes and getting your name across their newsfeed. Post regularly, making sure that you're posting engaging content that is not just filler content. You do not want to be putting out a status that doesn't interest anyone, thus defeating the purpose of posting so often. Find out when your connections and most LinkedIn users in your area are online and post during those times, the same as you would with Instagram. If you're getting more comments, shares and likes at one time than another, then post your status updates and information at those times.

Try commenting on other peoples' posts, engaging with them and making them aware of yourself and your brand. If you're not sure what to comment, just share the post, as this will get the same kind of awareness. If you can, and know the actual facts, answer on LinkedIn Answers, starting at once a month and then moving to once or twice a week. If you're jumping in and trying to start up various social media platforms and get as many followers as possible right away, it will end up a mess. Keep a schedule of things that you should do each week, such as invite one person to connect, comment and/or share posts, figure out how many times you want to post a day/week/month, and how many answers you will give out in LinkedIn Answers.

If you have a lot of connections, you are definitely bound to come across work anniversaries and new jobs on LinkedIn. LinkedIn will send you little reminders for you to help your connection celebrate their promotion, anniversary, or a new job. Take this opportunity to reconnect and give them a simple and courteous congratulations.

You can also try adding a Company Follow or LinkedIn Share button to your website, blog posts, and emails. This will get more people aware of your LinkedIn brand, bringing new connections your way.

TOOLS AND FEATURES

LinkedIn Premium

LinkedIn Premium can be a pricey upgrade for your profile. However, there are many perks that come with it. You have access to a larger photo and an expanded profile header, allowing your profile to stand out from others. You also have a gallery of images to choose from for your background, which is similar to how Facebook is set up to have your profile photo and your cover photo. With these three changes, your profile will become doubly noticeable when searches pull up results.

Besides making your profile more prominent, you will have access to the full list of those who have viewed your profile (up to the last 90 days since they have viewed). This is a great feature that can allow you to follow up with those who have searched for you and viewed your profile. You can send out a message to those who have viewed and not connected, or do a quick connect with them. LinkedIn Premium also allows for you to see the keywords that people use when finding you and your profile. For example, you'll be able to see where you rank on searches and where you should be focusing your money. When you see these searches, you can play around with your summary and profile to place these specific keywords throughout, bringing you into more searches by users.

For more targeted audiences and searches, whenever someone matches your criteria, you will also get up to five weekly e-mails. This can help you follow up with more leads and make more connections. You can also send out messages to those that you are not connected with using the open profile network, which is only accessible to LinkedIn Premium users.

Endorsements

Endorsements are found in your profile and let other users know what your particular skill sets are, and that others believe in your skill sets. Try getting connections to endorse you for skills by endorsing them first. LinkedIn is all about networking and a 'you scratch my back, I'll scratch yours' mentality. If you endorse your connections for their own skills, a lot will turn around and do the same for you.

Export your LinkedIn Connections

You've made connections via LinkedIn, and your connections are ready to receive newsletters from you and be kept up to date on your business. However, you have a lot of connections and taking the entire day to write out their information and then transport that information into another platform is no way to be spending your office dollars. You can actually export your connections from LinkedIn to another system by heading to:

- Connects
- Settings
- Advanced Settings
- Export LinkedIn Connections

You can now upload them into your own system and have those newsletters and updates sent to them from your office staff. This is also a great tool to use if you want to set up a schedule to follow up with your connections and see which ones turn into leads and leads into customers.

Keep in Touch

If you like the simplicity of using LinkedIn to keep up with your connections and stay in touch with them, you can also use this social media platform instead of your own system, which you may be paying for anyways. You can head over to the Keep in Touch button in Connections and make sure you do not forget to follow up with a connection or a lead again. Here, you can see when you haven't communicated in while, track your communications, get alerts when your connection has a birthday, job change or promotion. Always congratulate your connection on their new job, birthday or promotion as this can open up a fresh wave of conversation, initiating a stronger relationship between you two rather than just a connection on LinkedIn, getting lost in **the shuffle.**

LinkedIn Showcase Pages

These are a great way to target audiences and showcase your specific products and services. If you have some that may be of use to a younger generation, or to those in a specific area code, you can make a LinkedIn showcase page to cater to the specific target audience. Those who follow your showcase page do not necessarily haven't to be following your company page, so you're free to make it as specific as possible and use different creative outlets to try out different types of showcase pages. You can make ten showcase pages for your company, allowing you to branch out even further than just your original company page and newsfeed.

LinkedIn Pulse

Here, you can publish articles about the business world and your company, taking a few articles that you have already written on your own blog. This is a great way to get your name out there in the LinkedIn world and to promote your own blog or website. By offering snippets of articles or only the first two in a series out on LinkedIn Pulse, you can end up driving people back to your original blog or website. Make sure that your articles are concisely written with intrigue to pull the reader in and make them think about following you and your voice back to your company's website page or blog. If the articles that you are putting out there are not noteworthy or exciting, you won't be getting leads back to your website. However, if they're enjoyable and professional sounding, people will be looking to find more.

Problems with LinkedIn Advertising

The final social network that will be mentioned in this book in regards to social media advertising is the network of professionals or LinkedIn. Just like any other social media out there, LinkedIn has its share of problems that can prove problematic in regards to advertising on this social network. This social network provides you with the opportunity that few others are able to do. On LinkedIn, you are able to advertise your products or your services to a group of people for whom the products or services are intended to. With more than 364 millions of people using LinkedIn in order to build their professional network, LinkedIn is a great place to advertise your products, services or your company in general.

One o the biggest issues in regards to advertising on LinkedIn social network in connected to the click through ratio. In the case of this social network, only 1 out of 500 impressions or views will result in people clicking on your adverts. When we compare this to some other social network, we see the staggering difference. For example, on Facebook, 1 out of 250 views will result in clicking on your adverts which is 50 percent more successful rate than with LinkedIn and 1 out of 100 views on Twitter will results in clicking on your ads which seem to be the possible option for social media marketing. With this rate, it is hard for business owners to recognize the potential and importance of advertising on asocial network like LinkedIn.

One of the most important problems with advertising on LinkedIn is the price that you will pay for advertising. In the case of advertising on LinkedIn, you might actually pay from 1 to 3 dollars per a click on your ad. This seems likean enormous amount of money is your marketing campaign on LinkedIn turns out to be successful. However, with this being said it must be emphasized that LinkedIn also has one advantage that no other social media provide for advertising. When you are trying to sell a product or a service on LinkedIn, you target specific group of people for whom the product is intended for and when some of those people click on your ads on LinkedIn it is very likely that they will buy your product or your service. All this can lead to a marketing campaign that does not require any additional funds because it is able to finance itself through selling products and paying for the ads. Additionally, the LinkedIn offers only a few tools that you can use to manage your marketing campaigns on LinkedIn. Combining with the high costs of advertising, it may seem that the LinkedIn is not a very good environment for people to advertise your products and your services.

One of the biggest issues with LinkedIn is the amount of time you need to spend in order to fully use the full potential of this social network. It is very time consuming to navigate through all groups, connections, comments, answers and many other aspects. And if you do not have people dealing with these issues only, it will be very demanding for you to participate and fully use the LinkedIn. Regarding the advertising on social media, one of the crucial elements of advertising on these social media is your presence on that social media. If you are not online, you risk missing out on an opportunity that arose from a comment section on some social network, or you missed the question that could make a difference with customers regarding whether or not they will buy your products or services. One of the best tactics for using LinkedIn for advertising is to determine on which aspects your company will focus. In that way, you will be able to pay much more attention to those aspects, and you will not waste any time of trying to incorporate other aspects of the LinkedIn in your marketing strategy. Spending a lot of time on these type of issues may prevent you from devoting your time to some more important issues that may have an even bigger effect on your business, company or your personal life. It is important to develop a strategy that would reflect the company's needs, demands, and wishes in order not to get lost in the marketing strategies for your company. Although we previously mentioned that there are more than 340 millions of people who are using LinkedIn, this number can be somewhat misleading. Although there are more than 340 millions of people on LinkedIn the number of them who regularly log on and use LinkedIn is significantly smaller which results in the smaller number of people that you can reach with your marketing strategies. However, it is easy for you to see which profiles have been active on LinkedIn and which were not and with that information you can procede on placing your ads accordingly. With so many profiles that are not active often, it is not realistic to expect the benefits of advertising on LinkedIn in a short period of time. Instead, the benefits of advertising on LinkedIn come over a long period of time. As users log on to LinkedIn, they are introduced to adverts, and then they decide on whether to buy your products or services or not.

One common thing for all the social media out there is the question of privacy or rather the issue of having your profile open for all people to see it no matter how you set up the privacy settings. This is also the case with LinkedIn as well. Just like on any other social network, people can comment and like things you do. If you publish adverts on LinkedIn they become in the very moment you published them the subject of other people's comments. With that in mind, those comments can contain positive reviews as well as negative ones. While positive comments often improve the reputation of your business, company, your products or your service negative comments do the opposite things. Through negative comments, LinkedIn users might get negative pictures about your company and in that way, they perhaps will not buy your products or your services. In that way, you and the reputation of your business or company is reduced, and you have to able to respond to such comments. Otherwise, the reputation of your company might just continue to fall which will definitely be reflected on your company's income and the results.

As it was mentioned several times previously in this book, it is crucial to have people who know how to respond to such comments and to set the company's reputation back on the right and positive path. One difference between LinkedIn and other social networks regards the fake profile. Since LinkedIn is a network of professional who use LinkedIn to promote themselves and to look for better work opportunity, the number of fake profiles is very small, and it can almost be neglected. With that being said, it is important to emphasize that when negative comments occur on your ads, it is very important to take them seriously because they are coming from genuine people who might actually have problems with your products or your services.

Social Media

Another big issue with advertising on LinkedIn is the fact that you often get bombarded with request to connect with people who are more than often a sales agents of certain companies. After you accept their connection request, they start to offering a different kind of products or services. This, in fact, can cause people to have a negative opinion about the ads that appear on this social network. Since people previously bother with selling their products, they will think twice before opening certain ads that they see when they are using LinkedIn. Some of them might even try to find software that blocks the ads that they see on their pages all because they had negative experiences with people trying to sell them their products or their services. However, this supports the claim that when people once click on your ads and open them, they are pretty sure that they are going to buy your products or your services.

Another big issue is the fact that the LinkedIn is mostly used in conducting businesses between different companies. If you targeted group of people are individuals or customers then perhaps will have certain problems of finding new customers on this social network. On the other hand, LinkedIn seems to be the perfect place for big companies to their business among each other. Unlike big companies who look for a bigger number of clients (other companies), small businesses are devoted to individual customers and for them, it might get hard to fight through the ads of big companies and reaching an individual with those ads. Not being able to reach customers can be devastating to small businesses and because of that small businesses are forced to look for some alternative advertising strategies that are based on social media. The best solution for those kinds of businesses is Facebook because it provides them with the opportunity to reach a huge number of individual customers interested in their products or services unlike it is the case on LinkedIn.

Also, one of the biggest problems that the users of LikedIn who are trying to promote their products or service encounter is the lack of opportunity for the adequate promotion of your page or your profile. While on other social networks such as Facebook and Twitter it is much easier to promote your page or your profile doing that on LinkedIn is almost impossible. One strange thing in regards to promotion of your page on LinkedIn is the fact other users are not able to follow your page or rather LinkedIn does not provide them the option to follow.

One option for you if you want to promote your page or profile on LinkedIn is Linked Ads, but that will not do much in making your profile popular among the users. With this all being said, it is clear that it is almost impossible for a user promoting certain product or service to gain a big number of followers on LinkedIn. There is no possibility for you to invite other people to like or to follow the page of your company unlike on some other social networks.

Since the basic idea of LinkedIn is the connection between professionals as well as between companies and individuals, it is not clear why LinkedIn prevents people from connecting with companies they are interested in. And it seems that LinkedIn will not offer any improvement in the period to come. Without the possibility of being connected with companies of your interest, one may wonder what are the actual benefits of such social networks. Considering that companies are actually paying to have their pages on LinkedIn, it is even more striking that LinkedIn has made so hard for them to obtain followers or even if you want clients and customers.

With all this being said and no matter how big the problems may seem, LinkedIn is still one of the best choices if your company is switching to social media based marketing strategy. Although LinkedIn does not offer as many possibilities as Facebook or Twitter do, it still represents one of the most specific social networks in the work. LinkedIn being a network of professionals and companies, though following different objectives, is the great opportunity to target specific groups of people to sell your products or services. This, however, cannot be done on some other social network previously mentioned in this book. One thing that is clear is that there is room for much-needed improvements on LinkedIn that could benefit both companies and individuals as well as those small businesses who are trying to reach more people.

Chapter 8
Social Media Marketing Tips

Mine Twitter to Grow Your Audience While "if you build it they will come" is an incredible line from a motion picture, it's a bad marketing plan. To prevail on the Internet today, you need to make content that highlights and draws in crowds of people. If you are another blogger, you ought to invest more energy building up a group of people than making your product.

Here are three simple but neglected strategies you can use to gather a crowd of people on Twitter. Once you've been on Twitter for some time, you'll see that people will put you on open Twitter lists. Lists are arranged by specific interests or geographic area. For instance, I may be on lists for "marketing specialists," "bloggers" or "business instructors." Find a significant individual to follow, and after that dive into his or her rundowns. You'll likely discover a goldmine of intriguing people to follow who will ideally follow you back. There are numerous applications to help you find new supporters. One of my most loved spots to discover specific on followers is Twellow. This valuable and free site resembles the business directory for Twitter, and you can discover and follow specific clients for each classification, industry, and interest possible.

Platform

Use Twitter seek prompts. Open the desired ideal on the Twitter screen by following a couple of the prompts. This is a standout amongst the best statistical surveys accessible. Follow this connection if you need an entire instructional exercise on Twitter visibility. With these strategies, you can extend your gathering of people to contact people who are looking for your products and services.

Analyze Past Content to Improve Posts

Most companies examine the viability of their social media after they distribute. Presently, there are devices that break down information for content organization before you post. Here are the means by which you can use BuzzSumo to influence the information of what has been successful as far as social sharing. To begin with, enter a catchphrase that is a piece of your social media content. BuzzSumo will furnish you with a rundown of the top-performing content social shares as indicated by your catchphrase. Next, though some content performs better on one system over another, you can access any content from the social system. Furnished with this information, you can build the adequacy of your content organization by distributing content that has a better possibility of progress on a particular system.

You can likewise channel content by sort (which is perfect in case you're searching for recordings or infographics to use) or channel by day and age. The last gives you a chance to discover content that has been most well known in the most recent 24 hours or new content that has been popular in the course of the most recent year. The decision is yours!

Optimize Visual Content with Links

The visual content can go about as a "passage" to more significant content. At the point when arranging visual content to post on social platforms, think as far as how it can drive activity back to your site, products, and services. Interface a short video back to your site from your YouTube Account or your Instagram profile connection and ensure you give extended content around the video. What are you sitting tight for? Think as far as making passages to more profitable content when you arrange your visuals!

Maximize Twitter Real Estate With Images

"Consistently around 6,000 tweets are tweeted on Twitter (imagine them here on Internet Stats live), which compares to more than 350,000 tweets sent for every moment, 500 million tweets for every day and around 200 billion tweets for every year." Making an ideal tweet has never been more important. Adding visual interest to your tweet is an exceptionally brilliant approach to get your most vital content noticeable. You can add four pictures for each tweet or one big picture if you need. The decision is yours! To include various pictures, use normal Twitter. This is not accessible on any of the outside sites.

Switch Up Content Formats

In the course of recent years, I have moved to adjust the composition of my content for different platform to expand my breadth and visibility. For instance, by transforming one of my List25 articles into video consistently, I have become a popular YouTube channel to 1.3 million endorsers and have amassed more than 200 million video views. A comparable strategy with W beginner articles has developed endorsers of more than 8,000, and the channel has expanded deals for my WordPress modules. Changing content doesn't need to include just recordings. You can also turn pieces from your current articles into pictures—which have a tendency to have a better reach on Facebook. These pictures allow you to influence the force of other social systems, for example, Pinterest and Instagram.

Have you blogged much on one particular subject? Why not join those articles into a digital book and use it to assemble your email list? I you're not changing content configuration to enhance your success, then you are not improving your content to the maximum capacity.

Create a Social Media Channel Plan

Companies often feel overpowered by the need to make content for each social media channel on the planet. Alternately more awful is that many brands make one kind of content and after that, flood that content onto each social platform. If that is you, you require a social media channel plan. Your objectives are diverse on each social platform. Because of this, the content you create for that platform should be diverse too. Here are the segments for your channel plans.

The Channel (For instance, Facebook.)

The Persona (Who are you particularly focusing on? It would be ideal if you pick only one.)

The Goal (Is it a business objective, cost-funds objective or are you attempting to make a more client contacts?)

Essential Content Type (Textual, video, infographics?)

Structure (What does a general post resemble?)

Tone (Playful, snide?)

Channel Integration (How will this channel work with your different channels for best effect?)

Coveted Action (What are you hoping the clients will do?)

Publication Plan (Every channel needs its own article timetable.)

What's more, this is precisely why content marketing is not simple. If you influence a social media channel, plan accurately, you will have the ability to focus on the channels that work for you and be reasonable with your assets on alternate channels.

Deliver Content Consistently

An ideal approach to developing your following and engagement on social media is to be reliably present. The initial step is to set up the correct framework to keep your posts important, intriguing and profitable for your gathering of people.

Edgar permits you to make your own content classifications so you can monitor the particular sorts of posts you're discharging; this guarantees you do not overpower your supporters with similar sorts of posts again and again. You can likewise plan "rehash" posts indefinitely, so your content plan never runs dry. Additionally, Edgar permits you to transfer custom pictures for your Facebook, Twitter, and LinkedIn posts. As you construct your content library, upgrade your timetable with the classifications you need to post and when. At that point let Edgar deal with the rest.

Host Private Hangout On Air Events

Social media success is more regularly about having a discussion with the right people. Use a private group nearby standard Google+ Hangouts On Air (HOA) occasions, so you can have a committed, private party while having discussions with the right people. In doing this for our Academy, we've seen two patterns:

Around 33% of people watch the occasion during the day.

Around 8 to 10 people additionally join the occasion as members.

Not at all like with open groups, when you start your part inside a private one, the people get an party welcome/warning. This is a flawless approach to get through the commotion and contact the correct group of onlookers. In both situations, the occasion will be recorded under the Event tab, and also on the right-hand side of the group. The meeting is progressively individual, so eye to eye time with your group has a colossal effect. Additionally, the capacity to rapidly give them access to connections/assets brings about an awesome client benefit involvement.

Use Hashtags Strategically

If you need to be effective with your social media plan, stop irregular demonstrations of hashtagging and use a decent hashtag to tie the majority of the bits of your crusade together. Use a hashtag that is anything but difficult to spell and simple to recall. To ensure your hashtag is not being used for something else already, check for it on all channels before using it for your battle. When you make your hashtag, follow and join the discussion! To follow your hashtag, use sites like Social Mention and Sprout Social. Use TwiPho for seeking pictures on a hashtag.

Test Pinterest for Your Brand

A company that gives programming as a support of a group of people tried sticking their blog entries to

Pinterest. At times, the pictures from the blog entries were unique—infographics, their product being used or PowerPoint decks—and in others, they used a paid Shutterstock account. They constructed sheets with their image personas, speaking to five distinct portions, and got the chance to work. After only one month, Pinterest turned into their main social system referral source. The company's genuine objective was to drive people to take their free trial. In the previous four months, 35 people have come specifically from Pinterest and taken the free trial. Also, of those 35 people, ten have ended up clients. So a four-month trial of sticking blog entries to Pinterest has driven roughly $50,000 in new income. Not very shabby!

Use Social Updates to Write Blog Posts

Take your most mainstream tweets and Facebook posts, or the ones you feel most energetically about, and use them to create blog entries. You do not need to compose three pages; you do not need to even compose four passages. Seth Godin is a standout amongst the best bloggers in the marketing scene, and he writes in few sentence sections. He's an ace at communicating thoughts that are provocative and simple to peruse. People are in a rush nowadays, and content can overpower, so make it count and make it simple to peruse. Another approach to coming up with ideas is to remark on the things you read, for example, other people' web journals and bulletins, media productions and whatever else pertinent to your business. You're engrossed in the content and you most likely have suppositions when you're understanding it, so simply remark on those web journals. One advantage of remarking is that people will begin perceiving your name; another is it gives you material for a blog entry.

Give Context to Pinnable Images

We live during a time of data over-burden and limited ability to focus. With regards to catching your following of people's consideration, take the full favorable position of each risk to impart your message in a way that they'll draw them in! An ideal approach to picking up and keeping your group of onlookers' advantage is by utilizing viable visual content. Visual social media platforms like Pinterest can be an impressive movement source if used accurately. At the point when planning Pinterest design, ensure your pursuers know "what's in it for them."

Continuously incorporate the title of your blog entry on your picture. That way, when you stick it to Pinterest, clients will have an edge of reference and find a need to peruse it.

Become a Resource on Facebook

Throughout this year, Facebook has improved calculations that have guarded the number of people who can look at a Facebook page's post. These calculations can be used by page administrators to further build their visibility by considering their posts as client asset, instead of a tool. Manufacture a page that your clients would find useful and then use that platform to satisfy them. Write posts that teach, engage, interest and counsel to build a huge Facebook audience.

Manage Your Time Effectively

How long do you spend creating blog entries? Sending messages? Sitting in gatherings? Regardless of the possibility that you have an idea of where you're investing the greater part of your energy, you may regularly feel there are not enough hours in your day. Understanding time management is an enormous test for entrepreneurs. Attempt a time trackin device like Rescue Time to improve your day by day profitability and be more focused on the zones that need that focus.

For instance, suppose you invest a lot of energy associating on Facebook and Twitter, yet you do not see a considerable measure of results. In the interim, your email marketing effort is irregular, best case scenario, despite the fact that you know the outcomes are ready for whoever gets there first. Modify your day by day plan, so you invest energy in email marketing and check whether it drives deals. Keep in mind; computerized marketing relies on upon the trifecta of social, blog and email. If you disregard any of them, your whole system could endure. Notwithstanding, give them each a little love, and you may very well observe hazardous development. It's about finding the right adjustment that works for you and your business.

Expand Range Using LinkedIn Public

If you haven't effectively done as such, exploit the free content distributing highlight on LinkedIn called Publisher. It can increase your presentation to the interest group you have targeted and assemble your believability as a specialist in your industry. Truth be told, with LinkedIn Publisher it is possible to enormously broaden the extent of your business on LinkedIn, paying little mind to your system's size.

Every time you distribute, the greater part of your associations and supporters will be noticed. The post additionally has an opportunity to be incorporated into the email LinkedIn Pulse conveys to its people with proposals for posts that may intrigue them. To build your odds of progress with Publisher, make proficient looking posts that address the necessities and hardship of your group of onlookers. Ensure you abstain from including spammy or limited time data. Post profitable content that your system will impart to their associations and your span will become significantly more.

Focus on a Single Social Media Platform

Unless your company is a big brand, it's far-fetched that your clients are present in numerous social media channels. As such, to take advantage of your limited resources, find the one platform that has most of your optimal clients, and engage it like no other.

Computerize Curated Content

If you maintain an independent company, making or curating content can be consigned to the back burner. The issue is that an inconsistent distributing timetable can estrange your crowd and break trust. There's a route around this. Plan a benchmark of curated content. While there are plenty of tools out there that are helpful, recently I have been utilizing Hootsuite's new Suggested Topics that can be found under the Publisher tab. Select up to three subjects of intrigue, then let Hootsuite discover a content that is pertinent to your group of onlookers. As I said, this is standard content. If you need to shake your social media marketing, despite everything you have to make and minister your own particular posts, and also draw in with your group of onlookers. This app gives you a chance to stay before your following of people even when you're making deals, calls, composing recommendations, and fermenting that second pot of espresso.

Make a Social Update Library

One thing that keeps numerous companies away from effectively posting on social media is coming up with thoughts for what to post. When you group content and social media redesign creation, it's much less demanding to think of fascinating thoughts for announcements identifying with that content. At whatever point you create some amount of content (video, article or podcast) for your blog or website, make a list of 10 to 20 social media posts which can be used to promote that content.

This same idea will work for your item pages, deals pages or whatever other bit of content you need to advance. When you have a rundown of social media upgrades, add the overhauls to a spreadsheet to monitor them all in one area. This can be a straightforward spreadsheet that incorporates only the upgrade and a connection to the content, or it can be a more intricate one that tracks the majority of your content and social media overhauls for different systems. This will spare you a considerable measure of time as time goes on. Additionally, you manufacture a library of tweets and announcements that you can use for quite a long time to come. At whatever point you have to calendar a few upgrades, simply return to the spreadsheet, make a .csv record, import it into a program like Hootsuite and you're ready.

On LinkedIn, Publish Long-Form Content

By distributing new and already distributed content on LinkedIn, you have the ability to develop your viewers and system while enhancing your position as an expert. Through this open distributing platform, your unique content becomes a part of your company's profile, is passed on to the network you trust and can get the biggest gathering of specialists ever collected.

Target Those Who Visit Your Website Using Social Ads

You need to have push and a lot of investment to be able to draw in guests to your site. When you can pull in significant guests, it's critical to enlarge the potential of that visit even after they have left your site. There are currently awesome choices for retargeting in which you can direct your site guests to various places like Facebook and Twitter, and convince them to make more moves. For instance, to focus on your site guests on Facebook, show "page like" promotions and urge them to wind up fans. This at present costs us 15 pennies for every fan. Consequently, we get an applicable fan and somewhere else to contact our gathering of people. Your potential clients do not see the greater part of your correspondence, yet with great marketing strategies, you can enhance your odds of appearing in their social streams!

Chapter 9
Laws of Social Media Marketing

Utilizing the force of content and social media marketing can raise your group of onlookers and client base drastically. Beginning with no experience or knowledge could challenge you.It's essential that you comprehend social media marketing basics. From boosting quality to expanding your online passage focuses, keeping these ten laws will fabricate an establishment that will serve your clients, your image and - maybe above all - your main concern.

1. The Law of Listening Accomplishment with social media and content marketing requires all the more listening and less talking. Perused your intended interest group's online content and join dialogs to realize what's essential to them. At exactly that point would you be able to make content and start discussions that add esteem as opposed to jumble to their lives.

2. The Law of Focus

It's ideal to practice than to be a handyman. A very engaged social media and content marketing system planned to assemble a solid brand has a superior possibility for success more than an exuberantly costly technique that attempts to be all things to all people.

3. The Law of Quality

Quality always takes precedence over quantity. While it may be ideal to have numerous online acquaintants that read, impart and share your online content to their own groups of onlookers, instead of 10,000 people that disappear in the wake of interacting with you on the first run through.

4. The Law of Patience

Content marketing and Social media achievement doesn't just happen without any thorough planning. While it's conceivable to find a needle in a haystack, it's significantly more probable that you will have to focus on the whole deal to accomplish it.

5. The Law of Compounding

If you distribute stunning, quality content and work to manufacture your online gathering of people of value devotees, they'll impart it to their crowds on Twitter, Facebook, LinkedIn, their own sites and the sky is the limit from there.

This sharing and analyzing of your online content opens up new topic focuses for internet searchers such as Google to locate it in SEO searches. Those section focuses could develop to hundreds or a huge number of more potential courses for people to discover you on the web.

6. The Law of Influence

Invest energy finding the online influencers in your market who have quality crowds and are probably going to be keen on your products, services, and business. Interact with those people and work to manufacture associations with them.If you get on their radar as a definitive, fascinating wellspring of valuable data, they may impart your content to their own particular devotees, which could put you and your business before a gigantic new gathering of people.

7. The Law of Value

If you invest all your energy in the social Web straightforwardly advancing your products and services, people will quit tuning in. You should ensure that the discussion is entertaining. Put less focus on changes and more on creating outstanding content and forming associations with online influencers. In time, those people will turn into a capable impetus for verbal marketing for your business.

8. The Law of Acknowledgment

You wouldn't overlook somebody who contacts you in person so do not disregard them on the web. Building connections is a standout amongst the most critical parts of social media marketing achievement, so dependably recognize each who contacts you.

9. The Law of Accessibility

Try not to distribute your content and after that vanish. Be accessible to your group of onlookers. That implies you have to distribute content reliably and take an interest in discussions. Supporters online can be flighty, and they won't bother to swap you if you vanish for quite a long time or months.

10. The Law of Reciprocity

You can not anticipate that others will share your content and discuss you if you do not do likewise for them. In this way, a portion of the time that you invest on social media should to be focused on sharing and analyzing content distributed by others.

Chapter 10
Social Media Marketing Myths

Social media marketing has turned out to be inconceivably prevalent through the span of the previous decade; however, prominence doesn't prompt to change or refinement of a procedure. Inordinate prevalence has prompted to overhyping of the methodology; rather than concentrating on viable measures, genuine returns, and constraints of the technique, many have proclaimed social media marketing as some enchantment answer for quickly higher visibility.Social media requires a ton of research and diligent work, similar to whatever other marketing procedure. It's difficult to take in the intricate details of social media in the traverse of a solitary article, yet I'd get a kick out of the chance to begin by tending to - and scattering - probably the most widely recognized social media myths that keep entrepreneurs down:

1. **Social media is a business instrument:** If you need to get specialized, then yes, social media could be understood as a business apparatus as in utilizing it appropriately can prompt to more deals for your business. In any case, there's a confusion that social media is a monster sounding board for you to pitch your products, services, and self-serving declarations constantly. Consider your own particular utilization of social media- - do you sign on so you can read advertisements and listen to sales representatives? No. You go there to arrange, socialize, and find intriguing content. If your content is all deals

centered, people will begin to disregard your informing. This will bring about the natural reach of your presents on abatement, as the visibility calculations get on the way that no one truly thinks about the content you post. So keep sales content to a base and rather support important, significant, as well as social trades. For help making sense of what to post, see 100 Killer Ideas For Your Social Media Content.

2. Preferences and supporters are what genuinely matter. As advertisers, it's regular to attempt and legitimize everything with numbers. You have to gain an esteem higher than your expenses for any crusade to be beneficial, yet social media's esteem is to some degree theoretical. Accordingly, numerous beginner social advertisers swing to the main numbers they have- - measurements including "preferences" and "adherents"- - which they think straightforwardly relate with a crusade's prosperity. Be that as it may, remember that not everyone who "prefers" your image enjoys your image, and an adherent may not wind up understanding anything you distribute. Look for engagement measurements as opposed to these lighter numbers, and support the nature of your crowd over the amount.

3.Social media is a need, not a course for new clients.

A few business people see social media as simply one more thing you "need to do" in the cutting-edge time. Similarly, the same number of entrepreneurs have reluctantly consented to dispatch a fundamental site since every one of their rivals is doing it, numerous entrepreneurs have staked a nearness on social media- - however are not doing anything with it. To be effective in social media, you need to post effectively and frequently; something else, no one will see you, and no one will make a move by connecting with your image. Truth be told, this could hurt you; envision somebody who finds your image on Facebook, just to see who haven't redesigned your page in six months. What does that say in regards to your image's dedication to its open picture?

4. Social media is an autonomous system.

It's inappropriate to consider social media marketing as existing in a vacuum, as its own, autonomous procedure. It relies on upon various other computerized marketing procedures to be fruitful. For instance, without a solid brand, your clients will have nothing steady to react to. Without a solid content technique, you will have nothing intriguing to post. Without a solid site, any movement you create may very well ricochet. Social media is just a single part of a very much oiled machine.

5. Booked posts will take the necessary steps for me.

Post schedulers have turned out to be well-known apparatuses, particularly for companies whose social media work is a low need. There's nothing intrinsically amiss with them; post schedulers can be significant approaches to guarantee a base recurrence of posts, particularly on ends of the week when you're far from the workplace. do not use this as a substitute for signing on and posting progressively. It's called "social" media for a reason; you need to socialize with your devotees, in a two-manner discussion, if you need to succeed.

6. Social media is free, so I should accomplish something with it. Genuine, you do not need to pay to agree to a social media profile on general platforms. You can make natural posts without paying anything. If you regard social media

as a free component of your methodology, you will esteem it less; rather, consider social media as a speculation of time and exertion. Your time and exertion are important and the more you immerse your battle, the higher ROI you're at risk to see.

7. You need to "persuade" social media to be fruitful.

Excessively numerous business people have made the false presumption that social media is a youngster's amusement, or that you must be "aware of everything" to truly "get it." Do not get tied up with this. The essential start of social media marketing is basic; converse with your clients and demonstrate to them that you're a legitimate, dependable source. Try not to hand the procedure off to a university student since he/she's "young and they understand". Remember that more than 40 percent of Facebook's socioeconomics are beyond 35 years old, Would you believe another assistant with the entire oversight and administration of any of your other marketing techniques?

These myths are not harmless; if you become tied up with them, you could honest to goodness smother your advance or more terrible - contrarily impact the notoriety of your image. Still, do not be threatened by the universe of social media; since it requests a huge venture of time and exertion doesn't mean it's especially hard. Focus on the fundamental standards of drawing in clients, giving worth, and staying reliable in your image voice, and you ought to experience no difficulty growing a following.

Conclusion

Thank you again for downloading this book!

You should now have a good understanding of what social media marketing is and what some of the benefits are Chapters 3 through 6 gave you an in-depth look into Facebook, Twitter, Instagram, and YouTube. Each of these platforms can be used to increase your brand awareness and generate more sales. The skills you learned need to be integrated into your marketing strategy to build your online presence, build user engagement, and grow your business.I hope this book helps you reach your goals, and the tools provided put you on a path to success.

Finally, if you enjoyed this book, then I'd like to ask you for a favor, would you be kind enough to leave a review for this book on Amazon? It'd be greatly appreciated!

Social Media

Noah Hope

www.ingramcontent.com/pod-product-compliance
Lightning Source LLC
Chambersburg PA
CBHW070244190526
45169CB00001B/296